A Euro-American on a Korean Tour at a Thai Restaurant in China

*Perspective of an Adoptive Parent
of Korean Kids*

A Euro-American on a Korean Tour at a Thai Restaurant in China

*Perspective of
an Adoptive Parent
of Korean Kids*

Chris Winston

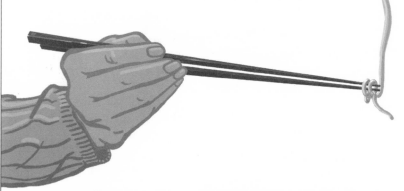

Korean **A**merican **A**doptee **A**doptive **F**amily **N**etwork
El Dorado Hills, California

A Euro-American on a Korean Tour at a Thai Restaurant in China

Perspective of an Adoptive Parent of Korean Kids

Korean American Adoptee Adoptive Family Network

P.O. Box 5585

El Dorado Hills, CA 95762

916-933-1447

www.kaanet.com

First Edition

06 07 08   10 9 8 7 6 5 4 3 2 1

Printed in the United States

Cover & Interior Design by Peri Poloni-Gabriel, Knockout Design, www.knockoutbooks.com

ISBN 13: 978-0-9776046-1-6

ISBN 10: 0-9776046-1-6

Library of Congress Cataloging-in Publication Data on file with publisher.

Dedication

To my husband, Mark,
for unwavering love and support.

To my children Alexis, David, and Diana
for inspiration.

To my mother, Barbara Hubbard,
whose perspective I have come to appreciate.

To Dr. Luke and Grace Kim
for sharing connections great and small.

To Dr. Eyoungsoo Park
for endless creative ideas and the best of friendship.

To Su Niles, and Jo Rankin,
adopted adults who shared your deepest feelings with me
at the beginning, when I had so much to learn.

To Kathy Beck, Maggie Dunham, and Terra Trevor,
friends and fellow parents of adult adoptees who have
walked this journey with me.

To all my Korean, Korean American,
and Asian American friends who have helped me
to better raise my children.

Table of Contents

Preface

The most important message of this book is that perspective matters. Because I have been involved in networking and community building as the president of the Korean American Adoptee Adoptive Family Network (KAAN), I have had exposure to a wide variety of individuals who are Koreans, Korean Americans, adoptees, and adoptive parents. I have come to deeply appreciate the differences in the way each of these groups and their individual members view the world and process their experiences with adoption. The processing is not the same, because none of us are the same. Throughout this book, I share parts of my own story as a parent of a child born to me and two children adopted from Korea, as well as the stories of others connected to the Korean adoption experience. Because each of us is unique, my story will be different than the stories of other adoptive parents, and most certainly different than the story of an adoptee, a Korean national, a Korean American immigrant or someone Korean American second generation, but our lives have common threads. It is through those common threads that we weave community.

While this book will focus on my experiences with Korean adoption, these experiences are transferable to interethnic adoptions from any country. Korean adoptions are part of the bigger picture of American families adopting children from other countries, which is a growing phenomenon. In fact, nearly 20,000 children are being adopted annually from other countries by American families. The majority of these are interethnic adoptions. While certainly there are cultural differences that make the experience unique depending on which country children come from, I believe the similarities are greater than the differences.

The first chapter of this book, "Beginnings," is included so that readers will have an introduction to members of my family whose experiences are included in subsequent chapters. Each of the following chapters focuses on one important issue that interethnic families face. These issues include perspective, racism, making ethnic community connections, being part of a strong and connected adoption community, the dynamics between birth and adoptive countries, meeting birth family, whether adoption gives adoptees a better life, and how to respect the boundaries between adoptees, adoptive families, and those from ethnic communities.

I have written this book for several audiences. First, I would like to share with fellow parents of adopted adults from Korea and other countries who have experienced some struggle within their families—those who sometimes keep that struggle to themselves for fear of being judged. I think that sometimes we are seen as the generation of adoptive parents before enlightenment who "didn't do things right." Of course, those who come after us can learn from us and do some things better, but I believe that there are certain elements, feelings, and issues that are inherent in the experience of intercountry adoption. There is pain and joy in raising any child. Raising a child of another race from another country adds layers of challenge that cannot be brushed off or avoided no matter what you do. I believe it is important that parents of adult adoptees have the opportunity to talk about their adoption experience and how it has affected them. In doing so we gain strength, find support, and make our experiences meaningful. This book is for my fellow parents of adult adoptees.

Second, in writing this book, I have had the opportunity to talk deeply with my own children and with other adopted adults with whom I share friendships. Many of them have told me that it has been helpful and interesting to them that I am willing to share my experience in a deeper way, because it lets them understand adoptive parents better. It is especially meaningful when that sharing can occur without anyone taking what is said personally, without our placing judgments on each other. This book is for adoptees who would like to understand adoptive parents better. I want adoptees to know how much I appreciate their willingness to share openly with me, which has increased my understanding of my own children.

Third, this book is for those who are prospective or current parents of young children adopted from other countries. Such a book would have been helpful to me in my journey. I hope that adoptive parents of young children will find this book helpful to them as they seek to listen to and relate well with their children, and as they seek to make connections to their children's ethnic heritage on their behalf. When parents adopt from another country, some have a theory about what they can do to support their children, some don't even have a theory, and most will find any theory difficult to put into practice. In this book I share the path I have walked and what I have learned, because while connections may be difficult to make, I believe that they matter. No matter what country a family is connected to, I hope that this book may make their path a little easier.

Finally, this book is for Koreans, Korean Americans, and Asian Americans who would like to understand adoptive parents better as they try to enter into supportive relationships with the adoption community. Around 100,000 Korean-born children have been adopted into American families over the last fifty years. They have been raised in all of the fifty states with varying degrees of connection to their ethnic communities and to each other. For many of them, it was an experience of isolation without connection to others of their ethnicity. Though connections have begun to be made, these connections do not always come about smoothly or to the mutual benefit of both the adoption community and the Korean American community. I would like to explore how these connections can be made more meaningful for both communities.

When Euro-American parents adopt children from other countries, their level of understanding of who they themselves are will be tested. Their capability in handling those obstacles that arise will be an important part of the adoption experience for their whole family. In this book all families adopting from other countries may find a bit of themselves, either as they are today or as they will be in the future. Because the experience of intercountry adoption is more predictable than it may appear, it is not wise to expect a journey without any ripples. Given that adoptive parents commit to this experience, perhaps they can use any adversity that they encounter to learn, to grow, and to become the best that they can be.

Beginnings

천 리 길도 한 걸음으로 부터

A journey of a thousand miles begins with a single step.
KOREAN PROVERB

Deciding to Adopt

As we rang in the New Year in 1987, I remained at home with my seven-year-old son, Alexis, in defiance of every college friend working with a master's degree or better. My plan had been to have two children three years apart, with the youngest in kindergarten, before returning to complete my education and enter the working world. Born to us, Alexis came so easily. I wanted more children, but my body hadn't cooperated. Somehow I felt incomplete and unable to move forward. My B.A. degree in psychology made me think of how Piaget had won the right to stay at home with his children by studying them. I studied my son, but only in my heart. I didn't want to alter my plan. Being a mother meant so much to me. Having grown up with three brothers, for me, one child wasn't enough to complete the idea I held of a family.

My husband, Mark, and I decided to adopt. Having a boy, we wanted a girl. The age of our child when she joined our family or her ethnicity didn't seem important. But we didn't know where to begin. We called El Dorado County's Social Welfare Department to attend an informational meeting on adoption, thinking our willingness to adopt an older child would ease the process. To our surprise, we were told an "older child" meant twelve and up, unless we did foster care. We wondered what all that "coming and going" associated with caring for foster children might mean for our son and for us. Seeing our discouraged faces, the El Dorado County social worker who ran the meeting suggested we call a private adoption agency. We called Children's Home Society of California the very next day, and we were told girls four to six years old were available. When we asked why, they said the children would come from Korea.

While he was growing up in Corpus Christi, Texas, my husband had a best friend, Jeff, who was of Chinese heritage. Jeff had a brother, John, and a sister, Jenny, both adopted from Korea. In their teen years, Mark and Jeff became interested in photography. I had seen many photos my husband had taken of Jeff's sister, a favorite model for pictures developed in their high school dark room. It felt comfortable to imagine a daughter who looked like Jenny.

Waiting

We began the home study process to adopt a little girl from Korea in February 1987. There were many steps for us to complete, including physical examinations, getting reference letters from friends and employers, meeting with the social worker for interviews, submitting details of our family finances, getting fingerprinted, and writing a personal autobiography. It took a few months, but we worked as fast as we could to complete all the steps. Our approval as an adoptive family came quickly from the adoption agency, with our paperwork being sent to Korea in July 1987. Then we began the wait for the referral of a particular child. It really was not a long wait, yet I could think of little else besides our daughter who lived far away. I cried a lot. This felt so much like our experience with infertility that it was hard to think of a different outcome, to hold a belief we really would have more children in our family. We seemed so bound by limits.

Her picture came in February 1988. Eun Jung Lee was one year old, not five, a beautiful smiling baby. She was Asian. For a second, I was surprised. Why? Perhaps it was my first hint her ethnicity might matter a little, not to us, but to her. As we had waited for this first picture of her, I read everything I could find about Korea. One was a book by Richard Kim, *Lost Names*. In the book, the author talked about how during the Japanese occupation of Korea, Koreans were forced to change their names to Japanese names. He talked about the pain of losing their identities. I worried about changing our daughter's name. Keeping her Korean name in the middle, we planned to wrap our name around it, knowing in gladness and in sadness that we were changing who she was.

We had to wait to travel to Korea to get Eun Jung, because our daughter had to receive a visa from the Immigration and Naturalization Service (INS) before she could enter the United States. Because the visa did not come within the expected one-month time frame, we believed something was wrong at INS. Miraculously, I talked my way into the office of someone with actual authority. The paperwork was lost. They were looking among stacks on the floor for February's mail, the timeframe of when our paperwork had been sent from our adoption agency. Unless they were willing to carry me out, I wasn't leaving. They called the adoption agency to have our paperwork resent. I intervened. "No!" I said, "I will bring it myself." The man was amazed I wanted to drive ten blocks. Didn't he realize I was willing to travel halfway around the world? "Be back before five o'clock," he warned me as I rushed out of his office. Not an hour later, I was back, paperwork in hand, and ignoring his parting shot, "Now you will give birth to one of your own." It was interesting how he seemed to believe that adoption cures infertility. It was not what he meant, but I felt in fighting for her she was "my own," and now she would come home.

Falling in Love with Korea

Alexis was ready to be a big brother. We went to Korea, and we fell in love. Alexis was delighted everyone wanted to have their picture taken with him. We didn't know why this was, but it happened repeatedly. Totally caught off guard, we were overwhelmed by the warmth of people toward us. Could a whole country consider you a guest?

One friendly Korean man takes a picture of Alexis with another Korean man in Seoul. Euro-American children were a rarity in Seoul in March 1988.

Before we met Eun Jung, the Korean social worker warned us, "She is shy with strangers; she will cry." But, she didn't. In my arrogance, I thought we had won her over, until later I saw the pictures of our meeting. We were given the gift of a gentle transition. In the pictures one can see frame by frame how a young Korean woman, who cared for too many babies, allowed us to greet our daughter slowly. At the beginning she had Eun Jung on the floor with her hands on our baby's shoulders. As we stroked Eun Jung's hair and gradually her cheek, the woman slowly moved away until she moved clear across the room, taking the camera from my husband, Mark, taking pictures of all of us. My daughter's eyes were like India ink, so dark one could not see the centers. They gazed at us with gradual acceptance.

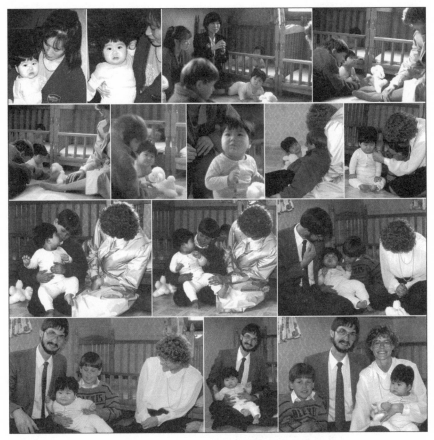

Meeting Eun Jung, soon to be Diana, at Seoul Babies Reception Home in Korea in March 1988.

Wanting More Children

When we returned home as a family of four, my son and daughter related well. Someone in Burger King cooed at Diana and offered her a balloon. Alexis put his face next to hers. "She'd like two." Alexis was a fountain of knowledge on Korea. Our daughter, who at age one was not crawling, bloomed with our close attention. Alexis and I began to talk at our adoption agency about how we went to Korea to get Diana. We encouraged others to think beyond an airport, to consider traveling to pick up their children. We had no information about Diana's birthparents. The only history we could give her were the pictures from our trip to meet her, frozen in a few moments of time, of her life in Korea. Korea was rapidly changing. It was a Korea that would not exist when she visited in the future. My sense of it was overwhelming. What would it be like to lose one's past?

In November 1988, we began the adoption process again as we wanted more children, and we hoped to balance the ethnicity in our family. Our social worker came to our home for a visit, arriving before my husband. When my husband arrived, our daughter jumped up and ran into his arms, "Daddy!" It wasn't hard to be re-approved.

But, things had changed. The Olympics came to Korea in the summer of 1988. Because of negative publicity about Korea as a country that "exports" children, adoptions from Korea to the United States had slowed. As the prospect of another Korean child joining our family dimmed, we waited and waited for the referral of a particular child. The adoption agency wasn't getting any referrals from Korea, and we were at the bottom of the list of those waiting. We reminded our social worker we were willing to accept an older child in the hopes that would make a difference.

In October 1989, with sadness because our hearts were in Korea, we asked the social worker to rewrite our paperwork for Vietnam. We were thinking if our new child could not be Korean, at least our daughter would have a sibling from Asia. On Friday afternoon, after I signed the documents to change countries, our social worker reminded me, "You cannot wait in two countries. After I submit these papers on Monday, you will be waiting for a child from Vietnam." As I left our social worker's office that afternoon I said, "If we get a referral from Korea today, we will take it." By 7:00 that night, it was a miracle; we had a picture of a five-year-old Korean boy named Sang Moon Yang.

Return to Korea

We agonized over who would go to Korea to get Sang Moon. Alexis, Mark, and I all wanted to go, but we could not imagine leaving Diana at home, even with relatives. After all, Korea belonged to Diana, and the trip was about family. International travel with our two-and-a-half-year-old daughter was difficult, but in December 1989, we all went to Korea with our daughter screaming practically the whole trip. I stood on a street corner in Itaewon and rocked her, a baby with her days and nights mixed up. A Canadian man came up to me, an adoptive father himself, and he said, "Sometimes it is best to go straight to the airport." I cringed. This was not my new child. In the back of my mind I wondered, did the sounds and smells make her think we were giving her back? In a better moment, she flirted with strangers on the train to Incheon.

One man with enough English asked, "Korean girl?"

When we said yes, he commented, "Very Western." It was not a compliment.

We met our five-year-old son, Sang Moon, who came with us willingly. When we gave him a new backpack full of toys for the plane ride, he sat in the middle of the airport, opening the backpack, and he wouldn't get up. But, when my husband and older son started to walk away, he picked it up and followed, chattering in Korean.

On the plane, we sat next to a Korean man who had just visited his wife

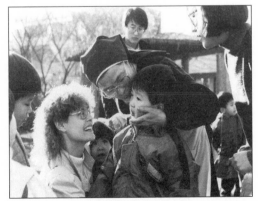

Meeting Sang Moon, soon to be David, at Star of the Sea Orphanage in Incheon Korea December 1989. Diana's face peeks through in the center.

and young children in Seoul. He was an immigrant, returning to a shoe business in Los Angeles' Koreatown to spend Christmas alone. Missing his family, he became an extended part of ours. Sang Moon sat between this man and my husband. The man translated our son's wishes and offered reassurances. As we approached landing our son started to cry; I felt helpless. Our helpful friend, with a soft comment in Korean to our son, reached over and unbuckled our son's seatbelt. In my newness as a mother, looking for entitlement, I did not reach over to rebuckle it. As we walked down the ramp off the plane, our traveling companion handed us a business card and said we could call him if we needed anything. He gently put his hands on our son's shoulders and kissed him on the forehead. It was like a blessing.

At Christmas time, I sent this man a card with pictures of our son, but somehow lost the address afterward. On April 29, 1992, two-and-a half years after Sang Moon arrived, the riots following the acquittal of police officers in the beating of Rodney King spilled into Los Angeles' Koreatown. Desperately I searched for the address of this Korean man, but could not find it. I couldn't remember his name, though I clearly remembered his face. Knowing more than 2,000 Korean businesses were looted and destroyed during the riots, I wondered if he was ever able to bring his family over, if he was all right.

Adjustments

David didn't have the words to tell us what he wanted for Christmas that first year, but we figured it out. He taped toy cars to the bottoms of his shoes, to indicate roller skates. He found an old car antenna and pointed it at another toy car. For Christmas he received the first in a series of remote-controlled cars he would save his allowance and do odd jobs for. He watched *Pinocchio* and pointed at the puppet's long nose. "Like Mommy!" he exclaimed. Did he think we were all liars? It was only the first in a string of "Disney moments."

I made a new Korean American friend, Chong Hui. I had walked into her dry cleaners and asked for help translating for my new son. In my ignorance, I believed if she spoke to David once a week in Korean that he would be bilingual. At the end of six months, we visited my friend's mother, our *halmonee* (grandmother), who spoke to our young son in Korean. David turned to me, "Mommy, what she talk?" I was thunderstruck he did not know.

David was a child without any competent language. I now know it has a name, subtractive bilingualism. His native intelligence was clearly well above average, but he had lost Korean and floundered in English when we attempted deeper conversation. It was like a learning disability that affected him for years. Mis-

Chris, Diana, and Chong Hui at her dry cleaners.

understanding each other, in our frustration, we fought often.

Alexis got quieter and quieter. David was watching *Cinderella* and commented on the stepmother, "I used to have a mom like that. Now I just have my favorite mom." Child of my heart, whenever we fought, I could play that tape in my mind to gain control. David began to avoid Asians. He said he was afraid "Mommy will be all gone." Remembering the orphanage, he said, "Koreans are mean." I was concerned about his self-esteem. Chong Hui visited David's orphanage in Korea. When she returned, she relayed conversations that convinced us both David was doing better emotionally than he had been while he was in Korea. It was small comfort observing what still seemed to be overwhelming struggles for him.

David, Alexis, and Diana in summer 1990.

Family

During our first four years as a family of five, it was clear my sons were different from each other —Alexis was very academic, David a social butterfly. I looked for ways to link them together, but it wasn't up to me. It was Halloween when David wanted to make a devil's costume with glowing eyes. When Mark became frustrated with the complexity of it, Alexis offered to help. The boys disappeared into the garage and re-emerged with a devil's mask glowing with red Christmas tree lights. Winning the costume contest, David split the coupons for junk food with his brother. I had no control over my sons' relationship. It had not always gone smoothly. But at this moment, I could see that they had connected themselves.

It wasn't only my kid's relationships to each other, but also ours with each of them that sometimes seemed out of control. When we adopted children from another country, we had unknowingly bought a ticket for the ride of our lives. There was the temptation when we came to a bump in the road to try to slide around it for fear of getting stuck, pretending it didn't exist, hoping our kids would ignore the bump too. But somehow, by the grace of God, we didn't do that. Instead of sitting in the shade under a tree watching our kids ride, we got on the rollercoaster with them. In doing so, we hit the bumps together full-on, smashing into the air, our lungs burning from a full-out scream at the height of the upward trajectory before gravity pulled us back to the ground. We had done a more difficult thing than we expected adopting children from another country. It brought us challenges. In the years that followed, we did our best to meet those challenges in ways that enhanced all of our lives. Often the path to a deeper relationship has been not to worry about control, but to see our interactions as a two-way street and challenge as an opportunity. Scary though they may sometimes have been, it has been the bumps in the road tossing us into the air that caused us to reach out for each other and hold on for dear life, leaving us more connected when we let go.

Like a ride at the amusement park, we have not been as out of control as it seemed, though our senses and our reactions have been stimulated. The experience has not been what we expected when we stood in line for the ride, with all the peaks and valleys hidden from our view around the bend, but it has been wonderful. In the pages that follow I share the ride our intercountry-adoptive family and others within the Korean adoption community have taken, the issues we have confronted, and the way that I have processed the experience.

Making Korean Connections

시작이 반

Starting is half the task.
KOREAN PROVERB

Multicultural Friendships

Over the years my family benefited from being around people from a multi-cultural background who value others as human beings. We made friends with other multiethnic families formed by marriage and adoption, enjoying connecting with other families whose composition seemed in some ways to mirror our own. There are many such families in the Sacramento area, the most integrated city in America, according to the cover story of the September 2, 2002 issue of *Time* magazine. Sacramento earned this distinction because people are more intermarried and inter-mingled than in most American cities. Early on I came to believe that to understand and deal with racism we needed to know other people of color. Through such friendships, I have increased my understanding of what it takes for those who are not in the ethnic majority to have a positive image of themselves. We were fortunate we were able to make such friendships naturally. We met people who had origins from all over the world, as fellow adoptive parents through the Hand in Hand adoptive family support group and as colleagues of my husband through his job at Intel. Not only did such friendships enrich our lives, but we were also able to find some sense of community in our diversity.

One special friendship was with Carmen and Pankaj. They entered our lives because their children, Jenny and Jason, were adopted from India. Carmen had immigrated to the United States from Venezuela as a child. Pankaj and his family had come to America from India. Through conversations with Carmen, I first explored the importance of multi-cultural connections and had beginning discussions of adoption issues. In 1990 as our preschoolers played at McDonalds, I remember Carmen sharing that they had considered adopting from both Latin America and India, but found their better and easier options for adoption in India. Because she was teaching her Indian-born children Spanish, we discussed her early concerns about her entitlement to do that, deciding their heritage through adoption ought to be as readily available as their heritage by birth. Their ethnic heritage by birth was there, of course, in the form of their father and his parents, who shared their physical features. In December 2004, Carmen wrote in their Christmas card, "Over the summer we worked in Peru. Jason and Jennifer worked in a squatters' settlement tutoring children in school subjects and organizing sports for them. Pankaj (he's a doctor) provided medical care at a clinic for indigent senior citizens, and I was his translator. These summer experiences have become what we look forward to each year, for the emotional rewards and the cultural immersion." Carmen and Pankaj are Americans and world citizens embracing all of their heritages. There are no better role models than Carmen's family. One might wonder why having friendships with families like Carmen's wasn't all that was needed for our children to grow to be productive confident adults.

Why was it important to make connections to my children's particular ethnic heritage? A couple of years ago at a Korean language class run by Friends of Korea, an adoptive mom asked a similar question. She had to drive a long distance to bring her daughter to our

Jenny, Jason, Carmen, and Pankaj in Costa Rica summer 2003.

Sunday language classes. She said, "I don't know why she wants to learn Korean. She won't have anyone to talk to. There is a Chinese language class at her high school. Her friends are Chinese. Why can't she learn Chinese and talk to them?"

David provided me with the answer, "Because she's Korean and not Chinese."

When my children were teased, they were teased specifically because of their Korean faces. They needed to know what it meant to be Korean American. As adoptees, they also had questions about their origins. Not only did they want to know about their personal history, about their birth parents, but they also wanted to know about their birth country. For our family's fulfillment as human beings, as citizens of the world, we enjoy a wide variety of multiethnic friendships. For a core sense of who they are as individuals and their unique history, I wanted my children to know about Korea, the land of their beginnings. That is how I ended up taking the steps resulting in an organization in Sacramento called Friends of Korea.

Finding a Guide

At first, it was difficult to make Korean connections because I didn't know how. As I mentioned previously, we were members of an adoption support group called Hand In Hand. Currently, Hand In Hand is a support group in Sacramento for families who have engaged in adoption of any sort. In 1992, it was support groups for those families with intercountry adoptions from any country in the world. I was the coordinator. Some of us with Korean-born children were trying to forge individual connections to our children's birth heritage in order to enhance their lives. Back then, this seemed unusual. I attended workshops at adoption conferences on interethnic parenting. All of those workshops were focused on Americans of European descent adopting African American children, but I felt the principles they espoused were relevant to Euro-American parents adopting Korean children. However, I was cautioned, "Koreans and Korean Americans will never accept your children. They will stigmatize them for being adoptees. You should be careful in interacting with ethnic Koreans." I wondered if any adoptive parent had ever tried to build friendships in their children's ethnic community. It was hard to believe other adoptive parents hadn't tried to make connections. Today I know some had, but those role models, if they existed, were not available to me.

Chong Hui, my friend who ran a Korean dry cleaning establishment, became my guide. I remember what a scary thing it was for me to introduce myself to her, but starting is half the task. I knew I was going to need help when my five-year-old son, David, arrived not speaking any English. Chong Hui wasn't very receptive to my overtures at first. She had once helped another such adoptive family, and the experience had not been a positive one for her. She felt they only wanted her to help their child adjust before cutting everything Korean from their lives. When I promised her we weren't going to do that, she relented.

Chong Hui provided an introduction to Korea culture, but also friendship. She taught me to make Korean food: *bulgogi, chapchae, bibimbap, kimbap, mandu, ddeok-guk*, and more, while her mother kept us supplied with *kimchi*. I bought a rice cooker, which is usually full of rice to this day.

I remember David's wonderment that I didn't know how to cook these foods he was used to—that I had to learn. Chong Hui especially earned my heart by reaching out to Alexis, my son by birth, making him a cake for his birthday. She wanted him not to be forgotten in all the "Koreanness." We spent a lot of time with Chong Hui's family. When Chong Hui needed to leave the dry cleaners for a doctor's appointment or a

Alexis celebrates his eleventh birthday at Chong Hui's house in January 1990.

school conference, I often went to mind the store for her. Sometimes my kids played with her kids in the back of the store while she was gone.

When in the fall of 1992 Chong Hui decided Diana ought to go to Korean School with her daughter Ruth, it seemed like a good idea. Ruth was Diana's age, and they really liked each other. Chong Hui made them green and yellow book bags with their Korean names on them. Chong Hui and Ruth met Diana and me at the school. The first day the stares we received from the other students were somewhat overwhelming, but we persevered. My daughter, then five, seemed comfortable with Ruth who served as her guide. Reluctantly I left, pausing at the entrance to the school where I bought a children's *hangul* workbook for myself. *Hangul* is the Korean alphabet invented by Korean King Sejong in 1446. I did not believe Diana could learn Korean by herself. Someone noticed my purchase. When I came back, the principal greeted me, asking if I would like to learn Korean. I jumped at the chance.

The adult class at the Korean School of Sacramento was small. Including myself, there were three adult students at the school among over one hundred children. One of the other adults was a Euro-American man married to a Korean woman; the other had lived in Korea. There were also second-generation students in our class. They were reading paragraphs. I struggled with the alphabet, working as hard as I could, with the irrational fear that if I did not do well enough, someone would ask me to leave. It was a fear that continued over the years in different forms as I struggled with my sense of entitlement, my right to pursue this connection for myself as well as for my children. Never before or since have I studied so hard at anything as I did initially trying to learn Korean.

For six months, it was a wonderful experience until internal politics led to a decline in the school's enrollment. Chong Hui decided to leave and take her daughter to language classes back at church. She had wanted us to attend church regularly with her before, but somehow it wasn't a good fit for me. We were comfortable at the school and decided to stay. Without her friend, my daughter floundered. Kids asked us questions. Pointing at me one little girl asked, "How come you are English and she isn't?" One day, two girls teased Diana because her mother was Caucasian. Diana cried for a long time. I didn't take her back to the school, but I kept going myself. I felt challenged to find a connection for my kids.

Finding Another Path

If we are lucky, friendships last a lifetime, but that isn't the usual course with many people we meet. Friendships ebb and flow, come together, and drift away. Chong Hui and her family moved across country. While we haven't lost touch entirely, life has moved on. Walking into another dry cleaner, barging into someone's life, didn't feel comfortable. I wanted to make real and reciprocal relationships. Of course, no one becomes friends with everyone he or she meets. It took time to find people I connected with. We had to have something in common. In my everyday life I met people who were involved with the organizations and activities I engaged in. It required my remaining in the Korean American community to find other people our family could relate to well enough to build friendships.

When Diana no longer wanted to attend the Korean School of Sacramento, I continued without her. Eun Young Kim became my teacher. Having previously been an instructor at the Defense Language Institute in Monterey, California, she was an excellent teacher. Eun Young taught me how to listen to context and make sense out of words I didn't understand. She taught me to sing innumerable songs that still hold much of the Korean vocabulary that hasn't yet fallen from my brain. It was a joy to study with Eun Young. Our relationship grew beyond language, and we became close friends. Her daughter, Yuna, was wonderful with children and became a big sister to my kids.

Chris learns Korean from Eun Young in spring 1993.

As summer 1993 approached, knowing school would be out of session until the fall, Eun Young asked me if I would like to study privately with her over the summer. Suddenly, I blurted out, "I really want to start a program where adoptive families can learn as whole families." Because in addition to being my teacher, she was also the vice principal, it was easy for Eun Young to go to then Principal Kahn and get his permission to make a pilot program for adoptive families. Upon receiving his permission, she told me we would need a group of five families. The entire Winston family was joined by the Goldberg-Lapointe family, the Winder family, the Artz family, and the Russell family as our fellow pioneers. The cost of the summer program was to be borne by the adoptive families.

Connecting to the Korean American Community as a Group

Diana's experience of being teased because her mother wasn't Korean in the second-generation classes at the Korean School of Sacramento, had convinced me it was better to connect to the Korean American community as a group of adoptive families, rather than individually. For six weeks in the summer of 1993, classes were held one evening per week on the University of California Davis Campus. Parents met in one room and learned basic language skills. The children met in another room and learned some language along with songs, dancing, kite making, and games. The kids ranged in age from five to eleven years old. As an end to this successful experiment, we held a party to which we invited extended family, community representatives, and the Korean language newspaper reporters. We asked the principal of the Korean School of Sacramento to request that the school board let us become part of the school as a special program beginning in the fall of 1993.

Eun Young and her daughter, Yuna, make mandu, while Father David Oh teaches Mask dance to kids in the pilot program for adoptive families held at UC Davis, summer 1993.

Since the Korean School of Sacramento held classes on Friday evenings and Saturday mornings, our program was to be held on Sunday afternoons. Our original five families plus the Williams family became the Sunday afternoon program for adopted children and families. As in our summer pilot program, there were separate classes for children and adults. All of the classes were held in donated space in a building housing a Korean Market. The market was owned by one of the board members of the Korean School of Sacramento.

Sunday classes for adoptees and adoptive parents needed to be different than the classes for second-generation children who spoke and read Korean at home. The teaching needed to be appropriate for students from non-Korean cultural backgrounds. The students did not expect to become fluent. Primarily, they wanted to experience language and culture. It wasn't possible for children in adoptive families with little or no knowledge of their motherland to know the minimum cultural expectations of them from their Korean schoolteachers. Adoptees didn't know the proper ways of showing respect to elders, accepting a gift with two hands, always greeting the teacher with a slight bow when entering or leaving the classroom, etc. Adoptive families needed the special care of being taught these things. Eun Young and the teachers she guided were willing to start at the beginning.

The hope was there would be, in addition to the Sunday program, special programs in dance, music, etc., where there was enough commonality for adopted kids and second-generation kids to join together in learning. That winter it happened. The adoptive families were asked to participate in the Korean School of Sacramento fundraiser, which was also a Christmas party. I was invited to a planning meeting for the fundraiser. As the only non-Korean in this environment, I was not as nervous as I should have been because it was fascinating. Some people were Korean nationals living in America. Some were Korean Americans. A psychologist, Dr. Eyoungsoo Park, was chairman of the fundraising committee. He asked if the adoptive parents would be willing to sing Korean songs at the fundraiser and buy tickets at sixty dollars apiece. It was not a request I could ever have anticipated.

How could I come through on this one? They each had to make their own decision, and these adoptive parents did not even sing in church. I was sure sixty dollars would be too much. As I hesitated, they dropped the price to forty dollars, especially for us. I felt shame. Though Eyoungsoo was challenging me, there was something about this man that made me know this was a legitimate request, something that felt like acceptance. Over time, I came to know him better, always valuing his intelligence and generous heart, and his eccentricity. Somehow, we all decided to buy the tickets and attend the fundraiser.

In segregation, the Euro-American adoptive parents congregated on one side of the room. Though their classes had been taught separately, all of the Korean American children, adoptees and non-adoptees alike, sang together as part of the day's entertainment. Mixed in with the second-generation children, the adoptees seemed absorbed into the community, as their parents stood out like sore thumbs. My eyes misted with tears. "Were we giving them back?"

The adoptive parents sang and the audience joined in with big smiles. In our singing, the Korean Americans in the audience seemed to find our acceptance of them. By joining our singing, they indicated their acceptance of us. The importance of singing together was an unexpected piece of Korean culture. I had prepared to say two lines in English thanking them for including us in the community which stretched endlessly in Korean. Taking on blind faith the word of Eun Young that this was an accurate translation,

Singing at the fundraiser for the Korean School of Sacramento at Christmas 1993.

I listened to a tape of her voice over and over, so I could parrot it correctly, "*Hankuk arini rul eep yong ah*...(Children adopted from Korea)" At the end the audience clapped. I had made a new friend. Eyoungsoo asked me to be a member of the school fundraising committee. I was asked to be a member of the school board as well.

Thunderbolt from the Korean School of Sacramento

After such a high feeling of euphoria from the fundraiser, we were caught completely off guard by the thunderbolt that struck in January 1994, prior to the new semester that would begin in February. A new principal, Mr. Kang, was in charge of the school, and he did not get along well with Eun Young. He began visiting the Sunday class and wanted to change it, because he was not happy with our style of learning. He gave the children instructions in Korean that they did not understand, repeating them more loudly in the hopes enlightenment would come. He took pencils out of the hands of the adults and criticized our handwriting. Particularly, he scolded Eun Young for not teaching us well enough.

Soon, he came to our Sunday class and fired Eun Young at break time in front of our families. In response, we wrote a letter to the school board of the Korean School of Sacramento. We tried to show our respect and appreciation for the school, while asking the school board to mediate the dispute between the principal and Eun Young. It was translated by Eyoung-soo and sent to the board. It wasn't long until Eyoungsoo called me saying we could take the program out of the school, find a new place to meet, and have Eun Young as our coordinator. I wanted to cry. I begged him, "Please don't let them push us out. Can't you find a way for us to stay as part of this community program?"

It wasn't until years later I came to realize the enormity of the task I had given Eyoungsoo, of the difficult position I put him in. Somehow he pulled it together arriving on the next Sunday with the principal. Principal

Kang and Eun Young shook hands. It was a miracle. Eyoungsoo had appealed to the principal not to abandon these children and families seeking connection to their heritage. A couple of weeks later, Principal Kang drove up with a truckload of used school books.

"Take what you want," he said.

We carted them off with great excitement. Peace reigned. We enjoyed the rest of the semester until summer break.

Part of the challenge we faced in our Sunday program was due to the background of the particular individuals on the school board of the Korean School of Sacramento. They tended to be older men who had held jobs of higher status in Korea than they did in America. Principal Kang, for example, was a teacher in Korea. In the United States, he was a struggling merchant. His past experience in schools from his native land was one in which the principal held absolute authority over the teachers, and that was his expectation. Eun Young on the other hand, who had taught at the Defense Language Institute and had a Euro-American husband, was more bicultural. It wasn't a good fit.

Parting with the Korean School of Sacramento

Over the summer the board of the Korean School of Sacramento looked at their budget, their need for a building of their own rather than rented or donated space, and the fact the Sunday program had grown to comprise one third of the school's enrollment. To manage us better they hired another principal, whose command of English was better, but whose heart was smaller than principal Kang's. There would be no more truckloads of Korean school books to choose from. We were told of the changes they would be instituting in our program. The new principal, Mr. Hong, decided all of us would listen to lengthy lectures in Korean history. Once again he was critical of Eun Young as was the school board. Mostly the Korean School of Sacramento wanted to eliminate the Sunday program, merging it with their other programs. "Korean kids are Korean kids," they said. "Adoptees should fit in and be Korean." They felt there was no reason they could not attend the Friday and Saturday programs.

We wrote more letters to the board of the Korean School of Sacramento which went unanswered. My husband, Mark, points out things often happen because of economics. Because our program was on Sunday, the school had to pay electricity and teacher's salaries for an extra day. I often asked Eyoungsoo to tell the school board I was willing to fundraise and assume the additional costs of the Sunday program. Mark feels this wasn't enough because the school was trying to acquire its own building. They wanted us to fundraise for the building not for an additional program.

Years later, upon re-reading the letters I wrote, I can see how they could be perceived as demanding. They were written in desperation. On the one hand, within Sacramento we had a Korean School struggling to take care of the needs of first and second-generation Korean Americans. Asking them to respect our needs as well was putting a burden on them. We as adoptive families needed to give to the community, not only take from it. I wanted to do that. On the other hand, we had a program that was like glass. When broken, it couldn't be put back together. It worked because we had a core of committed families. If that core was broken, we would scatter. In addition to the letters, Eyoungsoo made continued attempts to help the board understand our situation. I requested meetings that were arranged but became fruitless when no one, or at best an unauthorized representative, showed up.

On January 19, 1995, our letters were finally answered. Eyoungsoo's continued attempts to keep us in the school had failed. All of the families in our program received a letter from Principal Hong addressed to "All Sunday Class Students and Parents." The letter mentioned "changes were necessitated by letters sent to various members of the school's administration and the board of directors by a Sunday class student/parent Ms. Chris Winston." Another part of the letter said, "Her letters outline the special needs of the parents and children of Hand In Hand. They iterate a number of 'requests' the school must meet in order to ensure the continued enrollment of Hand In Hand members. Of course, the 'requests' are in reality demands as they give no choice to the school except to either accede or refuse them." The letter concluded with the words, "The school and I will miss all the students and parents of Hand In Hand, who choose to leave us at the end of this semester. We wish you all the best in your quest." I was devastated. From the beginning, I'd had what I thought was an irrational fear that I would be asked to leave the school if I didn't do well enough. Now it had happened.

The initial six families who made up the Sunday program at the Korean School of Sacramento had been pioneers. It was groundbreaking to think of trying to be part of a Korean American community. Those at the school never quite recognized the uniqueness of these particular families. After we left, the people at the Korean School went out of their way to try to find adoptive families who were less troublesome. They might indeed have been able to find families who were less troublesome, but those families weren't interested in attending the Korean School of Sacramento or in becoming members of the Korean American Community.

Forming Friends of Korea

In the spring of 1995, upon leaving the Korean School of Sacramento, we formed Friends of Korea. Rather than becoming an adoption support group, Friends of Korea became one of the organizations that make up the Korean American community in Sacramento. While the core of the group was comprised of adoptive families, the intent was to reach out to interethnic families, tae kwon do students, English as second language teachers, anyone wanting a connection to Korea for whom connection did not come easily. Rather than focusing narrowly on adoption issues, the goal was to interact with and relate to other Korean American community organizations. We saw ourselves as an extended part of that community. The first board members were primarily Korean American professionals. I became the president of Friends of Korea, Eyoungsoo became the vice president, and Mark made sure we became financially sol-

Vice President, Eyoungsoo, and President, Chris, meet with Korean American board members of the newly formed Friends of Korea in spring of 1995.

vent. Unique at the time of its inception, Friends of Korea became a model others in different parts of the United States could follow. That spring my article, "Building Bridges to Your Child's Ethnic Community And Why It Is Important," was published in *Roots and Wings* Magazine.

Language Remained a Focus

One of the first tasks was to form the Korean Language and Culture School as a Friends of Korea program. Eun Young became the principal. I remain grateful to Father Oh, who rescued Friends of Korea by providing

Anna and Joanna Oh participate in our Korean Language and Culture School in the fall of 1995.

space for our school through his Korean Episcopal ministry, and to his wife Anna, an attorney, for incorporating Friends of Korea. Two of the Oh's children, Michael and Joanna, became students, interacting well with the adoptees in the language program. Adoptive families have always been appreciative of those second-generation kids who have wanted to be in the various programs, especially when it led to the chance for individual friendships. For our family in particular, Joanna became big sister and an excellent math tutor for David and Diana. Anna was a wonderful role model for any woman. I enjoyed helping her with typing and phone calls in her office when she was short staffed.

In September 1996, Eun Young left, and Eun Mi Cho, a professor at Sacramento State University became principal of the Korean Language

and Culture School. In 2001, with Eun Mi's help, we were able to convince my children's high school to begin an independent Korean Language study course that met their high school language requirement. David and Diana have not become fluent in what was once their first language, but they have some basics in language and culture they have found useful on trips to their motherland. Eun Mi's son, Jason, became friends with David. They enjoy skiing together when Jason comes home from college.

Dr. Eun Mi Cho works on class schedules for Korean Language and Culture School in Fall 1997.

Friends of Korea no longer offers rigorous adult language classes. Through action by community activist Grace Kim and letter writing by me on behalf of Friends of Korea, Korean language classes are now offered through Sacramento City College. Children's language and lighter adult language classes continue at Friends of Korea's Korea Kids Club, where language is learned through, songs, games, and cultural celebrations under the able leadership of Denise Park and Young Seo Jang. These classes meet at the Sacramento Korean Presbyterian Church on Sunday afternoons.

Friends of Korea Discussion Group

Since its beginnings, Friends of Korea hosted discussion groups on Korean culture, history, people etc. Enjoying Korean movies together and gathering to discuss them was a fun way to explore Korean culture. People who were not part of an adoptive family came forward to learn about Korea and to get involved with the local ethnic community through our programs. Some of these were adult adoptees, business people, non-Koreans married to Koreans, ESL teachers, etc.

Adopted adult Su Niles and Dr. Luke Kim chat at a Friend's of Korea discussion group. Luke Kim shared information about Korean ethos such as Han and Jung.

Trips to Korea

Friends of Korea developed a Family Exchange Program. Since the summer of 1996, the exchange program has matched American and Korean families, hoping to help them make connections to each other. The program tries to match families by age and sex of children, so they can build a friendship. After staying with their Korean family, American

families share in a tour of the country. My kids enjoyed meeting their special friends, Jun Sub, Ji Hoon, Min Jin, and Hae Ran. Through these relationships, they were able to explore the differences in being Korean and in being Korean American.

Jun Sub and David wrestle in Seoul April 1997. Min Jin and Diana on Min Jin's visit to the United States in August 1997.

Heritage Festivals

Shortly after incorporating, Friends of Korea became involved in an International House Conference in Davis, California with a focus on

Korea. It included games, seminars, and food. From this event it became clear that adoptees, as representatives of the Korean American community, could be involved in not only learning about their birth culture, but in sharing Koreanness with other Americans. Friends of Korea began to have an annual booth at the Pacific Rim Street Festival, providing games and cultural information. A favorite activity involved writing the name of festival attendees in *hangul* on rice paper. In 1999, Mr. Chong Byun began teaching Korean drumming as part of the Korean School program. Friends of Korea's drummers and later a dance group performed at the Pacific Rim Street Festival and the California State Fair.

At the Pacific Rim Street Festival in May 2005. Eyoungsoo writes names in hangul at the Friends of Korea booth. Friends of Korea's Han Ma Eum Dance Group performs.

Community Event

Most years, Friends of Korea holds an annual community event. Although it's called a fundraiser, it doesn't raise too many funds. The importance of the event is that adoptees, adoptive families, Koreans, and Korean Americans all attend. It is a chance to feel part of an extended community. In past years, Eun Mi Cho helped the teachers plan a program showcasing the school. Everyone ate Korean food. Grace Kim often emceed the event, making it bilingual. The planning committee tried to choose speakers who could draw both the adoption community and the ethnic community. Over the years, speakers have included: Korean American journalist K.W.

Lee; venture capitalist
Chong Moon Lee; Con-
sul General of the San
Francisco Consulate,
Ri Hoon Hur; Educa-
tion Director of the San
Francisco Consulate,
Chong Ae Kim; Miss
Pennsylvania, adult
adoptee Susan Spafford;
Washington State Sena-

Mr. Byun's drummers pose with Miss Pennsylvania prior to a Friends of Korea Community Event.

tor, adult adoptee Paull Shin; and Korean Congressman Jay Yoo.

Service to the Korean American Community

I continue to believe relationships should be reciprocal. If the adoption community wants Korean American community support, it works well if the adoption community also supports the Korean American community. Friends of Korea continues to offer access to events sponsored by other Korean community organizations, encouraging its members to attend. Friends of Korea assisted with "Law Day" providing free legal advice to immigrants. English language practice for Korean American senior citizens has

Chris teaching English to senior citizens at the Sacramento Korean Presbyterian Church in fall 2002.

been provided. Friends of Korea members volunteer for health fairs for seniors sponsored by both the Korean Association and Sierra Lions Club. I am on the board of the Korean American Coalition, an advocacy group for Korean Americans.

Sacramento Korean Presbyterian Church

Friends of Korea Receives Support from the Korean American Community

Friends of Korea receives support from Korean community organizations as well. After a time, it was no longer feasible for Friends of Korea educational programs to remain at Father Oh's church. With the help of John Seo, Friends of Korea moved its programs to the Sacramento Korean Presbyterian Church in 1997. For years the church has not charged Friends of Korea any rent, have welcomed our usage of their building, and have greeted adoptees and adoptive families warmly. They have invited adoptive families to their events, but have never once engaged in any proselytizing. I have wondered what adoptive families could give to the Sacramento Korean Presbyterian Church. Friends of Korea makes small donations occasionally, but that is not why church members find sharing their space worthwhile. Seeing adoptees in the church at Friends of Korea programs gives church members a sense of pride. In their outreach to the adoption community, the church finds part of its mission in supporting adoptees and adoptive families in their connection to Korean heritage. Appreciation expressed by the adoption community touches the hearts of church members.

Every year the Korean Marine Corps of Northern California presents a check to the adoption community at their fundraiser. Mark and I enjoy this get-together. We are not good dancers like Mr. and Mrs. Chang, but I always sing a song in Korean at their event. Last

Mark and Chris sitting with Mr. and Mrs. Ki Ho Chang at the annual Korean Marine Corps Event December 2000.

year it was a duet with their president, Yong. S. Kay. Friends of Korea gets good support from the Korean Consulate in San Francisco.

Over the years, there have been hundreds of people, primarily from adoptive families, who have participated in one or more of Friends of Korea's programs. For those who want it, Friends of Korea can be a bridge to other Korean American community organizations in Sacramento and individual friendships.

Friends of Korea families at a picnic with Korean exchange families and Korean American supporters in summer 1997.

Keeping a Relationship with Korean School of Sacramento

Sometimes those in the community tell me the Korean School of Sacramento is once again restructuring. "Friends of Korea will come back," they say with hope. They feel what occurred was only because of a personality conflict. I have thought about it for years. Was it only a personality conflict? Was it cultural differences? Of course there were personality conflicts, and the events did play out in a cultural context, but a similar falling out and disappointment could have happened anywhere where individuals and groups relate. It didn't necessarily have anything to do with Korean Americans. Yet to me, it did. Because of the depth of need I had to make connections for my children, the loss caused me to look for deeper reasons to explain what had occurred. In actuality a simple explanation may suffice. In a recent conversation with Eyoungsoo, I tried to get him to identify what he felt had caused the problem.

He said, "They couldn't appreciate the particular needs of adoptees as different from second-generation needs. This was because they weren't capable of listening. You don't have those sorts of people in the adoption community?"

"Yes, Eyoungsoo, there are some."

I experienced deep feelings of loss on my kids' behalf and guilt on my own behalf, because of my experience at the Korean School of Sacramento. It was difficult for me to accept adoptees needed a separate program from second-generation kids because of who we, their parents, are and who adoptees have become because of adoption. If adoptees are in Korean language classes with non-adopted kids with Korean American parents, adoptees become perpetual kindergartners, as kids are placed by language ability levels. To have to accept we could not fit into this Korean School, whatever its own internal problems, even as a separate program, was heartbreaking because it involved accepting what my kids had lost through adoption. This is not to say Korean Schools in the United States are necessarily optimal at meeting the needs of second-generation kids either, or that non-adopted Korean American kids don't have losses due to their parent's immigration. That is not the point. I only acknowledge that being a Korean American kid with Euro-American parents is different than being a Korean American kid with even one Korean parent. In interethnic adoption, adoptees lose the ability to fit easily within their own ethnic community.

It took me years to realize and deeply believe being kicked out of the Korean School of Sacramento was not the same thing as being expelled from the community itself. Connecting with groups of Korean Americans can be emotionally charged, especially for adoptees, but also for adoptive parents of young children connecting on their children's behalf. When we are in a heightened emotional state, it is easy to over generalize any rejection, any inability to form relationship, to some flaw either within the Korean American Community or within members of the adoption community. It may be more useful to focus on what makes any relationship work.

Making Relationships Work

Let me share another more mutually satisfying group interaction. In March 2005, Friends of Korea, the organization we formed upon leaving the Korean School of Sacramento, worked on a community project with the Sacramento Sierra Lions Club, a club in which all the members are Korean American. In alternating years, Sierra Lions Club holds Korea Night. On Korea Night, Sierra Lions Club invites all their non-Korean American friends and members of their fellow Lions Clubs to this evening where all can experience Korean culture. It is important to Sierra Lions Club members to share their ethnic heritage in a way that is appreciated. To do this they need both dedicated Lions Club members, but also an interested audience. They asked Friends of Korea families to work with them to sell tickets and get the word out about the event. This gave adoptive families a valued role both in doing outreach and as appreciative audience. Additionally, Friends of Korea's Han Ma Eum dance group, which is composed primarily of teenage adoptees, and is currently our community's only authentic dance team, was asked to provide the entertainment. This gave Friends of Korea's teenage adoptees the chance to feel competent and proud in sharing their

Friends of Korea's Han Ma Eum Dancers perform at Sierra Lions Club's Korea Night in March 2005.

heritage. Our younger Korea Kid's Club children were asked to sing Korean songs, which included the younger kids and their families in the event. The reason the event worked was because it met everyone's needs. It met the needs of the Sierra Lions Club as they themselves defined them and the needs of the adoption community for inclusion in the extended Korean American Community in a way that felt comfortable.

It worked because of the relationship between Friends of Korea families and Denise Park and her niece Young Seo Jang, who are the teachers of our Korea Kids Club. Denise's husband, Kwang Seo Park, was the current Lions Club president. Our existing relationship gave us the tools to understand each other, know what the actual needs and expectations of each group were, and see that we would have our mutual needs met by working together.

Initially, we had been able to work well with the Korean School of Sacramento because of my relationship with Eun Young Kim and Principal Kahn. When Principal Kahn left, everything changed. The reason Principal Kahn left was the same reason I ultimately had difficulty. The majority of those who remained in leadership at the Korean School of Sacramento were not people adoptive families, or many Korean Americans, could continue to relate to easily.

Being pushed out of the Korean School of Sacramento ended up being an opportunity. "Adopted Korean American" is as valid a classification as "first-generation immigrant Korean American," "second-generation Korean American," etc. We were entitled to construct our own group on a par with other ethnic community groups. The flexibility and visibility within the Korean American Community that adoptive families achieved afterward would never have been possible had we stayed within the tight walls of the Korean School of Sacramento.

I have continued to attend annual fundraisers for the Korean School of Sacramento, while making financial contributions. Just as it is important to me that adoptive families be supported, I want to support a school meeting the needs of second-generation children. Not long ago, I was the only Euro-American person at the installation of their new chairman of the school board. At the installation, I was amazed to realize I knew two-thirds of the people in the room. I am connected to this community. It is right to care about community and the needs of non-adopted Korean Americans as well as the needs of adoptees and their families. There are those from the Korean School of Sacramento that I remember fondly. After all, they gave me my beginnings in the community and the chance to learn my children's first language.

The other day I visited the market building where our Sunday program was once held. The gentleman who owns the building and the market, and who was on the school board of the Korean School of Sacramento during the time our Sunday program was active, greeted me. He is retired, but still owns the building. He has always been warm no matter what.

"Happy New Year," he said to me.

"*Sae Hae Bok Mani Padu Sae Yoh* (Happy New Year)," I replied.

"She speaks Korean," he said proudly to his friend standing nearby.

"I learned right here," I said, "at the Korean School of Sacramento."

We both smiled. I owe much to the Korean School of Sacramento. It gave me the experience to really understand what my children have lost. It provided me with a remarkable experience to learn and to grow. However one's paths may diverge, it's nice to acknowledge those who have made a difference in one's life, to acknowledge what one has been given.

To Make a Friend Be a Friend

범굴에 들어가야 범을 잡는다

To catch a tiger, you have to go into the tiger's den.
KOREAN PROVERB

Going into the Tiger's Den

Adoption community members and also ethnic community members vary in the depth of their desire for connection. Some adoption community members decide participating in the Friends of Korea's programs are enough. In Korean culture, the tiger is a wondrous, courageous, and revered animal. As I was learning the language, I often was taught sok dams (Korean proverbs). Many of these proverbs were about tigers. My favorite became, "To catch a tiger, you have to go into the tiger's den." Its meaning is that to obtain something as valuable as a tiger, you have to work hard and take a risk. To make Korean friendships, I have entered the tiger's den multiple times to catch a tiger. I have always believed if my family had Korean American friends, my children would have a base if they wanted to connect with others of their ethnicity into adulthood. For my family and myself, I have wanted individual relationships with Korean Americans.

So, how does one make individual friendships? If a local adoption community has an organization like Friends of Korea, it can be a good place to go to begin to meet Korean Americans. In the case of Friends of Korea, it is the adoption community initiating the bridge. There are chances to meet ethnic Koreans at Friends of Korea's functions, but fewer Korean Americans will be found there than in their own organizations, because they are not as comfortable attending. Lack of English fluency and the underlying structure of events may make them hesitant. Only those who are brave enough to enter the tiger's den of the adoption community come to Friends of Korea functions.

Sometimes the outreach occurs in the opposite direction. I might get a call, usually from a Korean church, saying they will be holding a picnic on such and such a date for adoptive families. Usually the date is only a few days away. They may say, "Please bring forty people." This can be a difficult position for me to be in. I so appreciate the outreach to adoptive families. Sadly, in many cases such picnics are outside the comfort level of many adoptive families, as they are planned by church members in a way that is comfortable for their group, but not necessarily for the adoption community. They may want to know adoptees and adoptive families, but want to plan an event inside the language and cultural comfort zone of Korean Americans. They want to do something for the adoption community, but they want to be in control of what they are doing. In other words, they don't want to go into the tiger's den either.

Going Fishing

Korean American picnics, and also Friends of Korea activities, are places where those of Korean ancestry outside the adoption community and adoptees and adoptive families can fish for friendships with each other. Whether or not they are successful will depend on how many fish there are in the stream in which they choose to fish, and what bait they bring. I define "bait" to mean common ethnic heritage, common lifestyles, similar occupations, compatible temperaments, consistent motivations, the ability to meet mutual needs, etc. These are the same things that make any relationship successful. Some people may have to fish for some time without getting a bite because they have the wrong bait, leading to feelings of rejection and resentment. If a non-adopted Korean American and an adoptee or adoptive parent connect and a positive relationship develops, then they may have positive feelings about their relative communities. If they are uncomfortable going where the fish are or if they have the wrong bait, they may fish without success. Because the needs of adoptees, adoptive families, and ethnic Koreans for connection may be strong, if they have to fish for a long time or become uncomfortable quickly, negative stereotypes about each other are bound to develop.

Success at Fishing

One Euro-American adoptive parent, Kathy Beck from Seattle, was quite successful in fishing for individual relationships. When her daughter, Camille, arrived from Korea in 1987, Kathy connected with her fellow adoptive parents and adoption-related organizations in her community. Kathy was not aware of Korean Americans in her area, where they were, and what they were doing. She expected to rely on some sort of connections to the ethnic community through her adoption agency. When that didn't happen, she began to explore, ordering books and cultural items through the mail-order catalogs available at the time and visiting the Korean Consulate's office several times a year to pick up magazines and maps. Eventually, Kathy decided to find some Korean Americans. She did this by opening the phone book and searching under Korea and Korean. Although there were many listings, it was not easy to decide if and how to approach any of them, but it was the beginning of her search.

"I decided to call the Korean Artists Association." Kathy remarked, "Because Camille enjoyed art and was taking art lessons, I thought we might find out about traditional art, shows, and classes." Kathy was happy when she received a call back from the president of the association. The Korean Artist Association president was herself an artist, who incorporated many traditional techniques and images into her modern works. She invited Camille to participate in the youth competition that was coming up. Camille enjoyed the competition, which took place in a city park.

Youth were given specific assignments as to what to paint. "I planned on reading a book while Camille painted," Kathy said, "but I became more interested in watching the other mothers and their children." Kathy was surprised when the other mothers held umbrellas over their children to shield them from the sun, offering constant input with each brush stroke their children made. Kathy commented, "I looked over at Camille's sloppy water color and wondered—am I doing something wrong? Should I be exerting some control over Camille's work? Should I have sent Camille for specific training in Korean art?" Not being an artist herself, Kathy didn't see how she could make many suggestions for content or technique.

Camille seemed unaware her piece might not be considered appropriate for the expectations of the competition. She was quite proud when

it hung with the rest for a public display. It was clear the fact the Beck family was somewhat out of the parameters of the typical family participating in the competition didn't really matter. Camille considered herself an

Camille and her friend compete in the Korean Artist Association competition in summer 1995.

artist at an early age, and this was a fun way for her to experience a group event.

Kathy tells me Camille participated again in subsequent years. The last year she brought her best friend with bright blonde hair. Kathy was glad Camille continued to participate and was not uncomfortable her work didn't mirror that of the other participants. Camille felt comfortable enough being different in the group to bring her best friend to compete, even though that friend was of obvious Swedish descent.

Meanwhile, their artist friend kept the Becks informed about all Korean art shows in the Seattle/Tacoma area. She was faithful about picking up the phone and calling them, rather than relying on postcards announcing shows. On several occasions the Becks were able to attend openings and meet artists from Korea in person.

One reason Kathy was successful was she realized relationships work best when they meet mutual needs. Kathy spent some time figuring out what she could give to the artist association president. She tried to think of things that were actually needed not what Kathy thought she should want. What did Kathy Beck put into the relationship? Although she had performed a couple of small tasks over the years, it wasn't until the president began executing her dream of opening an Asian Pacific Cultural Center in Tacoma that Kathy saw an opportunity to really try to help her.

Kathy volunteered to be on the planning committee for the annual Lunar New Year's Celebration at the Tacoma Dome. She committed to weeknight meetings, even though that meant driving one-and-a-half hours in rush hour to Tacoma after work. Kathy told me, "Although I appreciated being exposed to their plan for the Cultural Center and being included in the event preparation, I truly felt like an outsider in the group." The planning committee was comprised of Asian Pacific leaders from the Tacoma area, none of whom Kathy knew except her friend. There were many conflicting needs and dynamics amongst the different communities, which Kathy couldn't even begin to understand. In the end Kathy understood what her friend would really like from her. Kathy was able to volunteer to get some press from the Seattle area and bring some event attendance from Seattle, in addition to manning a table during the event. It didn't seem like much, but it was the niche Kathy found that felt like a helpful contribution to everyone.

Kathy chose not to attend the weeknight meetings the following year, but focused on support that was really wanted. She helped by boosting attendance with friends from the Seattle area at the Lunar New Year event. The Center ultimately raised funds to purchase the former Tacoma Art Museum building. Sadly, the Center has not been able to sustain the costs of running the building and programs and recently sold the building. Kathy's friend is heartbroken. It had been her dream.

Kathy (left) and Camille (right) enjoy private Korean language lessons in 1996.

Another reason Kathy was a successful fisher woman was because she was willing to forge new relationships as time went on and relationships shifted or her family's needs evolved. When Camille was in fourth grade, Kathy had a growing feeling that in order to really feel comfortable in the Korean American community, her family needed some basic Korean language skills. "I telephoned one of the local Korean schools to determine if they had a place for us," Kathy said. The school put Kathy in touch with one of their board members, who was also a Seattle School District elementary school teacher. Sensing the Becks might not fit into their school structure easily, this teacher offered to give them weekly private lessons in their home.

Their private lessons worked out very well for eighteen months or so, but eventually this teacher became principal of the Korean school and had less time for outside interests. As principal, she worked very hard to develop a class for adoptive parents and their families. Although the Becks made an attempt to be part of the school, Camille did not enjoy being in a class with much younger kids, where she was placed according to her skill level. Will and Kathy also felt isolation in their experience of learning language separate from their daughter within the class for adoptive parents. "It was a real disconnect for our family after working together and supporting each other in our attempt to gain language skills," Kathy explained. "Sadly, we stopped attending."

Once again Kathy did not become overly frustrated when she had to look for new resources. After some additional searching of the phone book, Kathy discovered the Central Oriental Grocery was Korean-owned and only five miles from their house. Although small, in addition to housing a *kimchi* factory in their back room, the grocery sold all the mainstay ingredients for the dishes the Becks knew how to make. Song, Tai Ho and his wife and mother-in-law made all the *kimchi* sold under the Sun Luck brand at Costco, in addition to supplying restaurants and stores in the area. Mr. Song was the heart of their operation, with his wife acting as the backbone. "Mr. Song's heart was so big, he would've given away the store every day had his wife not kept a watchful eye on him," Kathy laughed.

Another reason the Becks were able to connect so well with the ethnic community was that they were able to set boundaries and work within their comfort level. Over the course of their early weekly visits Mr. Song asked the Becks many questions. He wanted to reach out to Camille to attend his church, asking if Kathy would drop her off every Sunday and let Mr. Song bring her home. This didn't feel comfortable to the Becks, and they declined the offer. By not becoming upset when Mr. Song offered opportunities that didn't feel comfortable, and by continuing to help him learn about their actual needs, Kathy deepened the relationship. "We continued to chat during our shopping trips," said Kathy. "On our visit to the store following our first trip to Korea, we went to see Mr. Song to tell him about our experience."

Mr. Song was a good fishing partner, because he also did not become upset when his ideas or overtures were rejected. He continued to listen for what the Becks might actually want and need. Picking up on the Becks' enthusiasm from their trip to Korea, he told them about the Northwest Chungchong Fellowship. The fellowship was a group of Korean Americans originally from Chungchong Province of which he was President. Mr. Song was bringing young people over from his home province and needed host families for them. He wanted to know if the Becks would be interested in hosting a couple of teens for two weeks.

The Becks quickly agreed, and soon they had two fifteen-year-old Koreans staying in their home. Their obligations included transporting their young guests to and from a central meeting point on days they had classes and tours, joining in group functions, and including their visitors in their family life. Although the Becks were the only host family with Euro-American parents, they were quickly included in group activities. Their instructions and meeting notices were not given to them in English, but someone always translated for them to be sure they understood. The Becks sat through many meetings conducted in Korean, show-ing up when told to, even when they had no idea what to expect.

Camille(left) and her parents, Will and Kathy(middle) enjoy visitors from Chungchong province in summer 1999.

"It was great fun," Kathy said. "The boys we hosted

were inquisitive and appreciative. The other host families were gracious and fun. We began to know their names, and discovered there was a large Korean American population in the Shoreline area, in addition to Tacoma." For the Becks, getting to know these families on this level increased their understanding of the community. Those they met came from all walks of life, but most were small business owners.

The following year, Camille was ready to explore her connection to her motherland without her family. She was asked to join the group of Korean American youth from Seattle going to visit Chungchong Province to stay with the family of a girl in Korea. Although she was the only adoptee in the group, Camille had a great time. She was happy they had included her.

Camille (right) in Korea with her friend from Chungchong province in summer 2000.

The Becks continued to host guests from Chungchong Province in subsequent years. Ultimately they were named honorary members of the Northwest Chungchong Fellowship. They were also asked to join the Korean Association, and they did. Kathy summarized, "Though meetings were held in Korean, and we were perpetually confused, we enjoyed attending events for both groups. There was always an 'I wonder what is going to happen' feeling in the air as we drove there." Picnics were huge productions with hot food and picnic games. Eventually, the Becks began to be invited to events at the Korean Consul General's home north of Seattle. As Camille got older, she was less interested in attending meetings where no English was spoken. In addition, their good friend, Mr. Song, was killed in a car accident in 2003. It felt like the heart of their connections to these groups was weakened without Mr. Song.

At age fourteen, Camille expressed a desire to continue studying the language of her birth country. Kathy and Will Beck knew at that point they would just hold their daughter back if they studied together, so they began investigating other options for her. Bellevue Community College had Korean classes at night, but youth under sixteen had to register with a parent for the class. Kathy called the school to determine if the class was appropriate for Camille. "Although my first preference was for her to find an experience where she could learn at her own speed, I was willing to register with her if I had to," Kathy said. The instructor telephoned Kathy. After some discussion, the instructor decided private lessons might be the best idea. She asked if Camille could find a friend to take the class with her.

Finding a friend wasn't difficult for Camille. Kevin Driscoll, an adoptee she met through culture camp and classmate of Camille's in middle school, was happy to attend private lessons with Camille. The lessons began on a weekly basis in the instructor's home, and ended only when Camille and Kevin headed to college. The instructor was a good support for Camille and Kevin. She was young, so she knew popular Korean music. She often shared food as part of the lesson. She translated letters as necessary for them. Although at times it seemed like they might have been having more fun than studying, Kathy thought it was the right environment for Camille to grow her language skills. While attending the University of Washington, Camille continues studying Korean. Kathy hopes Camille will find her college language classes a good experience.

In my experience, whenever members of different communities want to come together, the principles are the same. There ought to be a willingness to expand one's comfort zone, while setting boundaries when something doesn't feel quite right. Relationships work best when they are mutually satisfying and meet mutual needs. Those connecting with each other benefit by being good listeners. Each person can listen carefully to really hear the other party's needs, rather than defining those needs themselves. They can then determine if those needs are a good match. Relationships grow, diminish, shift, or change over time, so a willingness to form new relationships is important. Over-generalizing and stereotyping should be avoided when relationships don't work out.

Today, for adoptive parents who are reaching out for ethnic community connections, there are role models to follow. My friend Terra Trevor describes her positive experience of being connected to her children's birth heritage in her book, *Pushing Up The Sky*. Like Kathy and I, Terra made individual connections for her family. Like me, Terra also tried to make group connections, in her case between her adoption support group and a Korean American church. Whether the relationships are between individuals or groups, the principle of reciprocity and the path to connection is the same.

Working with the Resources Available

So what does one do if one doesn't live in California or Seattle? One works with the resources available. Of course, the more resources a Euro-American adoptive parent has, the more the children's life experiences can be enriched. However, as long as one is willing to expand one's comfort zone and reach out for mutually satisfying relationships, connections are possible no matter where one lives.

When adopted adult Mark Hagland was growing up in Milwaukee, Wisconsin in the 1960s and 1970s, his parents found a way to give him a small connection to other Asians. Mark Hagland had very, very little contact with Asian Americans and none with Koreans or Korean Americans. His parents, who were Americans of Norwegian and German descent, adopted Mark and his twin brother as their only children. Though Mark had loving parents, they had virtually no Korean cultural resources. There was no Koreanness anywhere nearby. In fact, Mark didn't meet a non-adopted ethnic Korean until his undergraduate college years at the University of

Wisconsin in Madison. He didn't have Korean food for the first time until his late thirties.

Yet Mark seems to have had a mother who was aware he needed connections. The closest thing Mark had to an Asian experience was Toy's Chinese Restaurant. Mark's mother worked at Toy's as a waitress during the World War II years and shortly thereafter to help support her parents and siblings and later herself. "Old Mr. Toy," the restaurant's founder, was fond of Mark and his brother. So, about once a year, Mark's parents would take their children to Toy's for dinner. Mark's parents were of extremely modest means, and dinner in a restaurant was virtually a once-a-year phenomenon. This dinner was special. "Old Mr. Toy," and later his son, "Young Mr. Toy," would treat Mark and his brother almost as long-lost relatives. Mark said, "I realize in hindsight the adults were very aware my brother and I had absolutely no other access to Asian people or culture, so this once-a-year ritual had significance beyond its surface meaning."

Whatever adoptive parents can do to make connections makes a difference. Despite living in areas with resources, both my fellow adoptive parent in Seattle, Kathy Beck, and I feel we struggled on our path to connection. If there are fewer resources, it might be easier for adoptive parents to avoid their own initial discomfort of connecting to Korean Americans, after all they have the excuse that no resources are available. It doesn't lessen the need. For our family, the more specific the connections have been to Koreans and Korean Americans the better, and the more my children have valued the connection. The more diverse we made our environment the easier our path became.

Adult Adoptees and Connections to Korean Americans

Over the years I have not been making connections in order to teach my children how they ought to incorporate Koreanness into their identity as adults. I had definite reasons for wanting to make heritage connections for my family. My purpose in doing it was to give my children resources and support for handling racism and identity issues. I see many positive ways those connections have benefited them in terms of their comfort level in being Korean American. They are using these resources to figure out what role Koreanness will play in their lives in the future. It is up to them to decide how big a part of their lives they want such connections to be. Once they became adults, such choices were up to them.

Whether or not adoptive parents make Korean connections, some adult adoptees will make connections to the non-adopted Korean American Community on their own as adults. One adopted adult I know, Chinook Shin, is a good example. She had limited exposure to her birth heritage as a child. In 1996, she was working in the California legislature as the secretary to the Senate Banking, Finance and International Trade Committee. Chinook had met other Asian Americans working for the legislature, primarily Chinese Americans. She was often invited to events for various Chinese American organizations and began to wonder if there were other Korean Americans, individuals or organizations, for which she could volunteer. One of the Chinese Americans she met gave her the name and phone number of Luke and Grace Kim. When the Consul General of Korea in San Francisco was invited for an introduction to the Senate by her committee, Chinook contacted Grace Kim. With Grace's contacts and assistance, Chinook arranged a reception for the Consul General and the local Korean American organizations. Chinook was interested in getting to know these organizations.

When the reception was a wonderful success, and it became known Chinook was an adopted adult, the ethnic community in Sacramento wanted to get to know her. She began to visit a different Korean restaurant each weekend, until she identified her favorite one. The restaurant owner, who shared her Korean last name and enjoyed her visits, began to share his challenges with her. Though his restaurant was one lot back from the main street, he had an

Chinook at an Asian American Event in Sacramento.

illuminated sign that had been visible from the main street through the parking lot of the gas station on the main street. The gas station had built a car wash tall enough to obscure the restaurant owner's sign. Chinook did research to try to find ways to confront the gas station about the problem. Though ultimately unsuccessful, the fact she cared and made efforts was recognized by the restaurant owner, and that in turn cemented their friendship. When Chinook traveled to Korea, everyone at the restaurant was interested and cared about her, almost like family. As a result of her friendship with Grace Kim, Chinook also became involved in teaching English to senior citizens and was loved by them. She became part of the Korean American Community on her own terms. Her Korean American friends are primarily first-generation.

Following his experience with Toy's restaurant, Mark Hagland also made Korean connections as an adult. The difference in his experience and Chinook's illustrates that for adult adoptees, making friendships with those who share their birth heritage can be achieved in a variety of ways. Mark said, "One interesting connection for me is that I have a gay Korean American friend here in Chicago. He and I share connections, both being gay and both being Asian American. He is not only gay, but also a one-point-five-generation Korean American, which makes the connection very comfortable for me." Koreans define one-point-five generation to be those who were born in Korea, but immigrated to the United States as teenagers.

After some thought, Mark also mentioned another connection. He told me about fifteen years ago, when he was editor of a magazine for physicians at the Illinois State Medical Society, he had worked with a second-generation Korean American woman. Recently, he was able to visit her in Cincinnati, where she is currently living. She told him she feels very isolated ethnically. "Cincinnati is very, very white," she told him.

"That reminded me once again of how second-generation Korean-Americans do have some things in common with adult adoptees," Mark said, "In fact I actually do have several second-generation friends."

Though Chinook and Mark have made Korean connections as adults, I also know other adopted adults who say having grown up without connections, the comfort level is not there. They don't feel the need to reach out to fellow Korean Americans. There is no one right way to be or feel. I don't know how my kids will feel ultimately. I think, though, that their childhood experiences will increase their options.

What about Korean Americans who want to reach out to adoptees and adoptive families? I asked Denise Park, one of our Korea Kids Club teachers, what she would recommend to those who wanted to make friends in the adoption community. She said, "I would tell them to go slow, don't be in a hurry. Don't ask a lot of personal questions, but be friendly. As in any friendship, keep an open mind and an open heart. Listen to hear what the adoptees or adoptive families really need, and then see if it is something you can offer."

"What do you get out of teaching us?" I asked her, "You are volunteering, we don't even pay you."

"If you paid me, I wouldn't be teaching," she said. I am not a professional teacher, but at Friends of Korea I feel what I have to offer is valued. Just being able to share something people are searching for has value to me."

For my family, having Korean American friendships as my children have grown has given my kids more opportunities to explore their identities as Korean Americans and to chart their own courses as adults. Whether adoptive parents want to connect to their child's ethnic community as individuals or in groups, they need to know it may take some time. Practice patience and avoid stereotyping. "To make a friend, be a friend."

Perspectives

우물 안 개구리

A frog in a well.
KOREAN PROVERB

Adoptee Perspective

Shortly after David arrived from Korea, our family attended a picnic for adoptive families in Stockton, California. It was a very early effort by Korean Americans to reach out to adoptive families in northern California. Korean students from the University of California at Davis were there sharing what they knew about Korean dancing and tae kwon do. Friendly and seemingly curious, the students mingled with various families headed by Euro-American parents gathered under the trees, playing Korean games such as *yut*, *jaegi*, and *kongi* with the little kids who had been adopted from Korea. The adoptive parents took pictures of the students clowning with the kids before everyone got in line for plates of Korean food mounded high, lots of *bulgogi* and rice, with a little *kimchi* on the side.

David and Alexis play yut as Chris watches, while Diana (center) poses with fan dancers at the Stockton picnic in May 1990.

At this picnic there was a lone adult Korean-born adoptee. Because she was not a little kid and appeared to feel awkward, she seemed to be searching for a comfortable way to fit into the event. Tentative, seemingly undecided if it was what she wanted to do, this adult adoptee accepted an invitation to sit down along with one of the adoptive families with young children to play games being taught by a Korean student. But, no sooner was she settled than it was time to eat. She got in the buffet line, and as they plopped rice onto her plate, Korean Americans tried to speak Korean to her. When she clearly didn't understand them, they seemed surprised. After they patted her sympathetically, suggesting she learn to speak in their native tongue, speculation began amongst them on whether she was of "full Korean blood." Oblivious to her discomfort, adoptive parents in the food line behind her peppered her with questions about how they ought to raise their adopted children. She responded with single syllables, suggesting she would rather not be quizzed. Becoming increasingly aloof and standoffish to the adoptive parents, this adoptee also moved away from those Korean Americans who tried to interact with her. She made no attempt to reach out to anyone, finding a corner off to the side, and turning her back as she ate her food. To the adoptive parents, it appeared she was being rude to the immigrant and second-generation Korean Americans who were being so sweet to the younger children.

A couple of us who were adoptive parents wondered to each other what her parents had done that she was like this. Somehow it was assumed right away that anything which looked awry must be due to her parents. Certainly, those of us with younger children did not want to make the same mistake in raising our children. We did not want them to grow up to be "angry." We were young families with young children. We still believed the ultimate happiness of our children was within our control. Though not one of us Euro-American parents was yet learning Korean or building meaningful personal relationships that would increase our children's ease and familiarity with Korean Americans, we still felt by "raising our kids right" we would be able to avoid all the inevitable challenges in the life experience we unwittingly signed up for when we adopted.

What never occurred to us was perhaps this young woman just had a different perspective on the adoption experience. While certainly her parents may have done many things wrong, they also may have done many things right. We didn't know anything about her family. Given the complexity of relationship and the life experiences surrounding adoption, her demeanor was not necessarily a comment on her relationship with her parents at all. In the years since that picnic, I have enjoyed friendships with many adopted adults. Through those friendships I have come to understand that adoptees have a wide range of comfort levels in attending ethnic community sponsored events.

One of my male adult adoptee friends expressed it this way, "I grew up not knowing any Korean Americans. Years later, when I was in graduate school, I began to meet Koreans and Korean Americans by chance, primarily through transactional contacts with taxi drivers, dry cleaners and florists. Those brief contacts were rather unsettling for me, as it seemed clear to me that culturally-Korean Koreans saw me as someone who was missing vital pieces of Koreanness."

The first interactions with ethnic Koreans he experienced occurred in the 1980s. Like those at the Stockton picnic, non-adopted Korean Americans he encountered had difficulty relating to him because of their previous limited interaction with adult adoptees. According to my friend, those Korean immigrants he met during that time period were universally shocked he couldn't speak their language. Some offered to have cousins or friends teach him the language of his country of origin. He told me, "Not being able to speak Korean was clearly a huge problem as far as they were concerned." There is a sizable ethnic immigrant community where he lives now. He does have access to it. But he confessed that despite having finally visited his birth country nearly three years ago, he still feels somewhat uncomfortable meeting Koreans and Korean Americans in social settings. He doesn't proactively explore what his ethnic heritage means to him, apart from occasionally reading books about Korean history and culture or watching subtitled films. To interact socially sometimes triggers his insecurities and brings back the feelings he has always had of being a "fake Korean"—inauthentic.

He said, "Visiting Korea three years ago helped me to feel more comfortable with my own 'foreignness,' if that makes any sense to others. Perhaps my interactions with Korean culture will never be deep or highly extensive. For many of us in the first generation of adult adoptees, the music of Korean culture and society will always sound like a 'hesitation waltz.'"

This adoptee is not the only adopted adult to share such feelings with me. From what he and others have told me, I can better understand what may have been behind the feelings and actions of that first adult adoptee I met at the Stockton picnic. She was at this picnic as the only adopted adult. She didn't fit well with the Korean college students, though she was also college aged, because she didn't know anything about Korea. Like the college students, this adoptee was Korean American, but her lack of knowledge kept her from being a peer in helping the college students teach the small children in the adoptive families. For her to be sitting with the adoptive families in a setting where all of the others of her ethnicity learning about Korea were children, put her as one of the little kids. Being an adult, this is not where she felt she belonged. Perhaps it also magnified her sense of loss at disconnection from her birth heritage. She was in what was likely a stressful situation from her own perspective on a life experience with inherent challenges that were primarily hers to resolve.

My impression was the older Korean immigrants who were interacting with her had different expectations of this young adopted adult than they did of the younger children. She didn't speak their language, and they were not comfortable conversing in English. Culturally, she didn't appear to have the skill set to behave in ways similar enough to their second-generation children to make them comfortable. They didn't appear to have the skill set to figure out how to reach out to her.

We, who were adoptive parents of the young children, were excited to see this adoptee, ready to pounce on her as a resource to tell us how we could be better parents. We didn't have the background to understand her ethnic identity might still be a work in progress, that this might be a rare opportunity in her world of few opportunities for making ethnic connections. She hadn't come to the picnic to meet anyone's needs, but her own. None of the rest of us attending the picnic had any idea what the world looked like to her. Each of us only saw it through our own eyes. It was unfair to make any judgments about her from this one situation. All of us at that picnic were people who wanted to connect to each other in one way or another, but none of us knew how.

Korean American Perspective

The first generation Korean Americans at the picnic had their own perspective, which seemed to include an element of guilt. For one thing the food at the picnic was being provided to the adoption community free of charge, without any expectation of reciprocity. Members of the ethnic community were expressing gratitude to adoptive parents for adopting Korean children, which felt uncomfortable to adoptive parents, because it seemed to imply adopting children was a charitable act. Through the eyes of Euro-American adoptive parents, the implication seemed to be that Korean Americans saw adopted children as having less worth than children born into their families. A more frightening thought was that they were thanking adoptive parents for adopting Korean-born children, because they viewed it as a temporary beneficent act, not a lifelong commitment. From the perspective of Euro-American adoptive parents, the implication could have been that because of their shared ethnicity some Korean Americans see the adopted children as more connected to ethnic Koreans than the children could ever be to their adoptive parents.

In his dissertation, *Comforting an Orphaned Nation: Representations of International Adoption and Adopted Koreans in Korean Popular Culture*, adopted adult Tobias Hubinette from the Department of Oriental Languages, Stockholm University, makes the case that the way Koreans feel about adoption can be found by looking at their media reports, films, music videos etc. His study looks at four feature films and four popular songs in analyzing Koreans view of adoption.

I have encountered other windows on Korean perspectives as well. One Korean American once shared with me his emotional reaction upon viewing a film of Korean children boarding a plane for adoption in the United States. "It feels as though the aliens landed and just snatched them up," he said.

Other Korean Americans have said the opposite, "They are so lucky."

I am quick to reply, "No, I am the lucky one."

What do Korean Americans mean when they say these things? Hearing such statements has made me wish there were a way to truly see how individual Koreans and Korean Americans process their interactions with adoptees and adoptive families. What judgments are they making about adoptive families? What judgments are they making about themselves? Relying on my interpretation of what I think I am hearing Koreans say doesn't allow me to understand what Koreans really think and feel. I know they have their own complexity of feelings about adoption that is deeper than it appears on the surface.

Birth Parent Perspective

I encountered birth parent perspectives unexpectedly. Immediately after David arrived from Korea, my husband, who worked at Intel, gave me a connection to Prodigy Computer Service for Christmas. In December 1989, the Internet was in its infancy. This "super highway" of information was unique and special. Eagerly I logged on looking for others who might be sharing my experience. I found few of them at first. There were no moderated, special-focused lists with opinions and participants who were screened for membership. Adoption bulletin boards were wide open. As I read through these boards, my eyes were opened to the fact adoption means different things to different people. Innocently I went to the Internet expecting to find adoptive parents talking about the joys of raising their children. Even though I could repeat to you any number of phrases about how adoption involves loss, the impact of those phrases had little depth of meaning to me. On Prodigy, I found birth parents expressing the raw emotions of loss.

What I found on the Prodigy network were American birthmothers who still felt traumatized over the loss of children they had placed for adoption thirty years before. They were not saying they had made loving adoption plans for their children as I had expected, but that they had been pressured or tricked into relinquishing their children. I found adoptees who felt a right to their history, and who were breaking laws to unseal their

Maggie (center) with her daughters, Kathleen and Jen (front) and Liz (behind) in early 1990.

adoption records. I found loss and anger that unsettled me. I processed these feelings with Maggie Dunham, the only other person I found on Prodigy who was a Euro-American parent of Korean-born kids. Maggie and I made friends with the birthmothers we encountered on Prodigy and learned from them. Commonplace now, though very rare then, together Maggie and I discussed what role Korean heritage would play in our children's lives, comparing programs she was involved with in New York with those I hoped to develop in Sacramento.

Perspective

Things are not what they seem on the surface in the relationships between adoptees, adoptive parents, Koreans, and Korean Americans. The most important aspect of my journey as an adoptive parent was the first step—the realization that my angle on the adoption of my children was not a universal view. While gaining this awareness, I sometimes experienced frustration and misunderstanding with all my fellow adoption community members and with Koreans and Korean Americans. This was not a one-time realization, but is an ongoing process of finding ways to step outside myself and see what those who are in a different position within the adoption community are seeing.

This is a book about perspective, in particular my worldview as a Euro-American adoptive parent of Korean-born children. My perspective also includes my perception of what adoptees, birth parents, Koreans and Korean American are experiencing. While commenting on my perception of what the mindset of adoptees, Koreans or Korean Americans may be, I only do so through the window of my own adventure as an adoptive parent of European ancestry. If I attempt to describe a world only each individual can see, I expect to be corrected by adoptees, Koreans, Korean Americans, and even other adoptive parents, and non-adopted siblings of adoptees. While our experiences have commonalities, they are also distinct. I appreciate those who are brave enough and willing enough to share their outlook with me, even if they do so loudly, trying to penetrate the thickness of the walls that surround me. I don't want to remain a frog in a well whose whole world is the walls that surround him and a bit of the sky. Without the deep realization that perspective matters, no amount of my "trying to do things right" makes up for the initial loss of respect for each other that occurs when I, and those around me, cannot acknowledge that each of us has a different view. Agreement about what that difference in view means for the Korean adoption community as a whole may not be nearly as important as the willingness to have an open respectful conversation about what each person sees because of his own unique slant on the panorama before him.

Letter to My Son

The following letter to my son David was first published in *Adoption Today* Magazine in July 2000.

To My Son,

I think of you, the little boy named Sang Moon, who came to our house from Korea, five, almost six years old. I remember your first English word was "7UP." You were so happy that when you said it, we immediately filled your glass with that sweet liquid—that is until we felt you had had enough and said, "No more." You threw the glass into the sink shattering it. Oh, then the battles began. I remember wanting to help you fit into your new world. I remember your resistance, your self-containedness, full of your survivor skills. But, we made it through, and one day I said to you in amazement, "We never fight." And you replied, "It is because I know how you think." I realized it was true for me too. I know how you think.

The other day we went shopping with the Korean Exchange Students who were staying with us, and they watched us in horror as you, your sister and I devoured the candy apples with a gooey texture and flavor so unfamiliar to Koreans that they would not touch them. I smiled at you and said, "There are some advantages to being American." I remember your calm reply, "I can do both." And indeed the image of you that very morning with Jun Sub, eating your *kimchi* and ramen for breakfast, floated back. Always that is what I have wanted for you—that you could do both.

I know you will continue to figure out how Korea fits into your life, what it means for you to be Korean American, how you can handle the missing pieces in your identity. I hope that along the way, you will continue to talk about it with me, that we will continue to watch movies like *Mulan* and discuss what it does or does not say about being Asian. I still look forward to watching *The King and I* and *Snow Falling on Cedars* with you.

Yet somehow I think the person you are, the boy who would join the high school snowboard team after only three times on a snowboard, will be what determines your life path. I will remember the math class where you came home shocked at getting a "D" when you were trying so hard. I remember trying to console you with the fact you had such a difficult teacher, telling you of other students we knew who had struggled in his class. I remember your statement, "He's not giving me an 'F.'" I remember your smile when you got your "B+." I am so very proud of you.

You know I have always liked it when each of you three kids was just the right size to fit snugly right under my arm as we walked. It is that stage between childhood and the teen years before you take off on your own. You remember the other day when I mentioned your sister, our youngest, no longer fits under my arm. You came over in your tall, almost sixteen-year-old height, put your arm around me and said, "Mom, you are finally just the right size." I knew then your need for me will continue to grow less and less, but our relationship, while it may change, will always be close. I will continue to enjoy watching you grow, so glad that in such a large world we found each other.

Love,
Mom

When my children arrived from Korea, I began to experience life as the adoptive parent of Korean-born children and a son born to me. It was evident from the beginning that my son David's—then Sang Moon's—perspective on his experience was different than mine. It seemed as though he felt he had been dropped on Mars, leaving all of us to figure out what limits should be set for him. What was he doing because of his cultural background? What was he doing because of his individual personality? What was he doing because he was scared to death? What was he doing because he was a normal little boy looking for boundaries? What was he doing because of having lived in an orphanage? What was he doing that should be respected and cherished? What was he doing that should be confronted and changed for his personal welfare?

In some ways my confrontations with David were just classic childhood struggles. In other ways they were battles of more depth than might be apparent. In our first four years together David and I fought a lot, almost daily. I wanted him to trust me and accept the limits I imposed, while he wanted to fend for himself in whatever way he felt was best. We were trying to get to know each other from backgrounds that were miles apart. We had to work to bridge the gap, until we came to understand each other. In the letter I wrote to him, I made note of a conversation we had one day when I realized we were no longer fighting each other. In the letter he said to me, "I know how you think." This simple statement made by my son triggered a realization that it was also true for me. I knew how he thought. Of course that is only true on the surface. I couldn't fully understand his experience, or he mine, but on a deep level we had a realization that each of us saw things differently, and that it was okay. We had respect for each other. Though his adoption experience remained a world apart from mine, each of us came to recognize the way the other thought—that we each had right to our own view. I wasn't going to tell him the world as he perceived it didn't exist. I had learned the importance of perspective.

Some folks have said what our family did in terms of reaching out to our children's ethnic community was only needed because we adopted an older child, but I don't think so. Though it may not have seemed like it at the time, David's ability to assert himself was a gift to all of us, especially to his Korean-born sister, in terms of broadening our perspective. Because of David's being the person he is, he was able to confront us. His need being in the open enabled us to make the connections we needed both for our family, and for other adoptive families. Ultimately, the understanding gained benefited the work of adoption community network building as well. The importance of the letter is the feeling of respect for each other that remains between us most of the time.

Our Different Perspectives

As the years went by I met adult Korean-born adoptees, and Korean birth parents. Often I found their feelings to be not so different from those expressed by the American domestic adoptees and birth parents I had met earlier on Prodigy. They were not the same, however, but had an added element that came from their experience as people of color.

I met Koreans and Korean Americans and found they brought their own emotional reactions to their experiences with the adoption community. Over the years I came to realize I could be a good listener, perhaps understand some of their feelings, but I would never know what it was like to stand in their shoes any more than they could stand in mine. It was not a matter of seeing adoption from the "proper" perspective, but realizing we can each only see it from our own perspective.

There is a catch phrase "walk a mile in my shoes" that invites us to look at life through someone else's eyes. It encourages us to realize other people, depending on their cultural background and life experiences, see the world differently than we do. It implies that if we open our eyes and ears we can see the world as someone else sees it. Such an attempt at sensitivity is a good thing, of course. My life has been enriched and broadened by placing myself into situations where I have had to stretch my level of understanding. Somewhere along the way I realized standing in someone else's shoes, let alone doing so long enough to walk a mile, is impossible. Perhaps the round-trip lesson from my attempting to walk from one place to another and back in someone else's shoes is to gain a limited understanding of that person, ending with the realization that the fullness of knowing the experience of someone else can never be obtained. Thinking I fully understand someone else's view can be as dangerous as not trying at all. Yet, I don't want to be a frog in a well. So, I do try to look at the world as others see it, always trying to remember to have the humility to know what I think I see may not be what I actually see.

Finding Ways to Stand Outside Ourselves

The reader will have heard the phrase, "A fish out of water." My husband, Mark, says a fish is not aware it is swimming in water until it jumps out. He had one betta fish that committed suicide in just this fashion, because no one found it quickly enough to render assistance. Jumping out of the water is certainly scary, but for most of us, it is not fatal. As a Euro-American adoptive parent I have often been unaware I was swimming in water because I seldom had to jump out. I was often not aware of the American culture, majority privilege, financial security, and adoption view surrounding me.

This lack of awareness can prevent Euro-Americans generally, and me specifically, from understanding that adoptees, Koreans, and Korean Americans are also swimming each in their own waters with a unique composition unlike that of those from different backgrounds. Maybe, this keeps adoptees, Koreans, and Korean Americans from clearly seeing my perspective as well.

No matter who we are, those of us who are brave enough can find opportunities to jump out of the water surrounding us. It is only by doing so that each of us has some chance to become aware of the surroundings we take for granted. It is very hard to get outside of ourselves. Like the fish out of water, we may find ourselves gasping for air when we do so. Yet, I believe we are all stronger and better contributors to our world after we have made the leap. It may be hard to find the opportunities to jump out of the water, but they do exist. We have to look for them.

For the adoption community in particular, without taking the risk, Euro-American adoptive parents do not grow and their families suffer through diminished relationships. Without taking the risk Koreans and Korean Americans may relate to the adoption community in ways that are not fruitful, perhaps even counterproductive to their intentions. Without taking the risk, adoptees may not have the chance to resolve the challenges in their life situation. Without taking the risk the adoption community may not provide the support that is needed for any of its members.

Racism

제 얼굴 더러운줄 모르고 거울만 나무란다

Not knowing his own ugly face, he blames the mirror.
KOREAN PROVERB

My Son's Teacher—Racism at School

In second grade David came home from school and told me they were learning a song he didn't like in music class. It was a song from Disney's *Lady and The Tramp*. The song is sung by two Siamese cats and goes, "We are Siameeiz if you pleeiz. We are Siameeiz if you don't pleeiz. We are former residents of Siam. There are no finer cats than we am." The song is sung in accented inaccurate English. After the song some kids were putting their hands under their chins and bowing to my son. I couldn't reach the music teacher, so I spoke with the principal. She listened to my concerns, spoke with the music teacher, and assured me they had moved on to other songs and wouldn't be practicing this one anymore. So you can imagine my annoyance when a few weeks later David came home and told me they were singing that song again in music class.

I went down to the school and was waiting to see the principal, when I noticed a Japanese American acquaintance, soon to become a friend, in the parking lot. Karen was second-generation Japanese American and her kids, who were half Caucasian and half Asian, also attended the school. I shared what had happened with her, telling her that not being Asian, I wasn't sure how to best support my son, and I would value her advice. I asked her if to her the song was offensive. She was very thoughtful about it and told me she had mixed feelings about that song. As a child in a school assembly she and the only other Asian American child in her class had done a dance dressed as cats to the song. She told me she had loved the attention, and the audience had cheered and clapped at the end of her performance. She said it was only now as an adult she understood why she had also felt uneasy about her performance. Having one's ethnicity appreciated as cute is not always comfortable. She asked if I would like her to come with me to speak with the principal. I quickly agreed, glad that our paths had crossed.

The principal welcomed us both into the office. She knew us well, as I was PTA president, and Karen was very active in the PTA. The principal told us she had done some investigating while waiting to see us. The reason they were singing the song again was that it was part of a multicultural day being planned by my son's second grade teacher, a well-loved faculty member at the school. The music teacher had not selected the song, but was having the children practice the song David's classroom teacher, an educator of many years, who'd had training as a "multicultural mentor," had chosen.

Karen began our discussion by pointing out that a multicultural day is an opportunity for children to experience the cultures of other countries. Karen noted Siam was now called Thailand. Then she asked a couple of questions, "Do you think this song is sung in Thailand? Do you think people in Thailand would be proud to hear this song?" Karen offered to teach the kids a Japanese song herself, noting multicultural days are more authentic when people share firsthand experiences from other countries. Through hearing about such experiences children can develop a sense of appreciation of those who look different, speak a different language, or have a different culture than they do. They can learn to treat those who are different from themselves with respect. The principal seemed to understand and was supportive. Perhaps she realized we weren't going away, and letting us have our way was the best damage control.

Then the principal called in the multicultural mentor teacher, who kept telling us the song was so cute. We should just see the kids singing it, and we would change our minds. She said the other kids liked my son and had just bowed to him in fun. She said I had overreacted. When Karen and I stood our ground, David's teacher relented, as it wasn't going to be too good if we pulled our kids from the program, being as visible as we were at the school. With my being PTA president and backed by Karen, the school didn't know how much trouble we might be capable of making.

It soon became clear David's teacher had not understood what Karen and I had been saying. When the multicultural day arrived, Karen and I attended with our children. Suddenly we discovered the entire program consisted of Disney songs caricaturing countries from around the world. I felt like I was stuck in the "It's a Small World" ride at Disneyland. Because our understanding of the multicultural day had evolved slowly, Karen and I had not yet realized the program included songs from continents other than Asia. In the multicultural program there were many songs. Only one was a real song, sung and appreciated in the country it was supposed to portray. Because of Karen, the kids learned a song from Japan. The teacher had not relented in replacing the song about Siamese cats with the Japanese one because she agreed with us. She had relented in order to keep the peace. She was not able to generalize what we had told her about Asia to other continents.

This teacher was, as I said, well-loved. Most parents fought to get their kids into her class. At the beginning of the year I had requested my son have her. Everyone saw her as an excellent second grade teacher, who was tolerant of challenging children, particularly boys who were a bit immature, helping them to fit well within her classroom. My son had only arrived from Korea a couple of years before. It seemed like she would be a wonderful teacher for him, and on some levels she was. She was Euro-American, would never consider herself racist and would not want to be racist. I am likely the only parent who requested her child not have her as a teacher. When I did so a couple of years later in regard to my Korean-born daughter, I made that choice with sadness.

Once again I was reminded of the Korean proverb, "A Frog in a Well." I was disappointed in my own limitation in finding a way to help this teacher climb out of her well and look at the situation from my son's standpoint. She just could not do that. This teacher remained stuck, like the frog, seeing only stone walls and a patch of blue sky. She was not being passive-aggressive. She really could not see how isolated and different my son felt when the kids sang a song that disparaged his ethnicity. Though well-meaning and a member of the ethnic majority in the United States, this teacher did not understand the privileges being in the majority conferred on her. Certainly she did not understand what it feels like to be a person of color in this country.

At the end of the multicultural program, Karen said something that changed my core understanding of how to handle racism. She said, "It has been great fighting this with you. I have really enjoyed it, but taking on racism in El Dorado County is a daunting task. If you are smart you will give your children some armor. Teach them about Korea. Give them their Korean heritage. Make sure they know Korean Americans. If they know who they are and have pride in themselves, such incidents will be less hurtful to them." I learned it is right to try to make a difference in society, nothing wrong about that, but if one is fighting racism against Asians, it is best to follow the lead of someone Asian. As a Euro-American adoptive parent I needed to acknowledge the world around me as it really was and give my children adopted from Asia survival skills. I was not going to be able to intervene in every instance of racism, overt or subtle, my kids would face. Likely I would not know about most of them. Euro-Americans cannot be role models for children of color in handling racism. Korean adoptees need to know other people of color and other people of their particular ethnicity well enough so they can lean on each other for support.

Racism Within Adoptive Families

If Euro-American parents are complacent about their perspective, the relationships with their adopted children suffer from the parents' lack vision. I believe most children are adopted into families where they are loved. Far fewer are adopted into families who understand what it feels like to be a person of color. I know I wasn't prepared. My son had a well-educated, caring, second grade teacher who exposed him to ridicule because her vision was limited. Like this teacher, out of their own ignorance, Caucasian parents and siblings, extended families, and adoptee's Euro-American friends, all have the capacity to make children adopted from other countries feel isolated and different.

Often parents do realize their children are going to face some racism. Not having experienced racism themselves, their expectation is that it will take the form of ethnic jokes, racial slurs, or harassment. While adoptees do experience those things, most of the racism my children have faced has been subtle, often from ignorance, not blatant and perhaps more insidious because of it. If someone hurls an ethnic slur or commits a hate crime, people of all races may rush forward in support. It is easy to understand the harm in such occurrences. Certainly my children have had friends who have stood up for them at such times. It is those other times when their friends have not meant to be hurtful, saying something in ignorance, and then refusing to acknowledge or understand what they have said or done, that my children have felt isolated. It happens for adoptees within their own families. If we wonder why adoptees may have anger about this, perhaps Euro-American parents have to look at their own ugly faces and not blame the mirror.

Asian Parents of Asian Children

Asian resources available in so many forms in California are wonderful. The Asian adoptive parents whose Korean-born children participate in our Friends of Korea activities are a special resource. I spoke with the Asian parents of teens who come to our Friends of Korea Han Ma Eum dance group, because I wanted to know what they did to prepare their children for racism and how they handled it when it occurred. Debby Staley, who is Chinese American, and her husband Mike, who is Euro-Amercian, have a son and a daughter, both adopted from Korea, who are in our dance group. The Staleys agree their children have not experienced racism, but it is not by accident. They have carefully chosen to live in neighborhoods where the makeup is thirty percent Asian. Mike's brother's wife is Hispanic, so at any family gathering the dinner table may hold a variety of foods from tamales to fried rice to hamburgers. The children's friends' ethnicities are wide-ranging. Their Korean heritage is available to them through Friends of Korea. They live in diversity.

Andy and Twila Noguchi are both Japanese American and have a daughter in our dance group who is adopted from Korea. Andy is former president of a chapter of the Japanese American Citizens League in Sacramento. Andy has long been an activist for civil rights for Asian Americans. Twila described an incident their daughter, Annie, experienced in first grade.

A boy in Annie's class came up to her pulled his eyes backward with his fingers to narrow them and asked, "Why do your eyes look like this?"

After some thought, Annie put her fingers above and below her eyes and pulled them apart making them rounder and asked, "Why do your eyes look like this?

I asked Twila, "Why do you think Annie could calmly think to do that?"

Twila answered likely it was because from the time she arrived from Korea as an infant, Annie had accompanied her parents to gatherings where Asians are in the majority. She had heard her father, Andy, speak many times about civil rights. They had been teaching her about Asian American history. Twila also mentioned that some months after this incident related to eyes, an older boy confronted Annie on the playground and teased her for wearing a T-shirt with a girl in a kimono on it. Annie cried when she told her parents she had kicked the boy and run away. Because her mother had praised her so much for how she handled the first incident, Annie felt she had disappointed her mother because she had not handled the second bully as effectively. Annie's parents let her know there would be incidents like this throughout her life, and the bravest adults are not always successful in how they manage them. The important thing, they told Annie, was she should never let anyone make her feel inferior.

As I listened to the Staleys and the Noguchis, what struck me was they had thought about racism before their children joined their families. They didn't expect they were going to change the world in areas with Euro-American majorities to their comfort level. Debby and her Euro-American husband, Mike, had researched where they would live very carefully. The Noguchi's were ready to share stories from their own childhoods and to provide their daughter with pride in being Asian. Neither family expected eliminating racism from the world would be the primary means of protecting their children. Instead they expected to set up a situation where their children could operate from a position of strength. This could be done by

We are fortunate the Friends of Korea's Han Ma Eum Dance group includes Asian American adoptive parents. Andy Noguchi (far left rear) Twila Noguchi (2nd from the left), Debby Staley (furthest front) and her Euro-American husband, Mike, (behind the drums).

selecting the right geographical location for home and school and by giving their children pride in who they are as a source of inner strength. What they have done in raising their children sounds remarkably similar to the advice I had been given by my friend Karen after our school's multicultural day. The more intercountry adoptive families isolate themselves from others of their child's ethnic heritage, the more challenging they make their journey.

Our Family Deals with Racism

After the multicultural day, the realization had sunk in that racism was not something our family was going to easily avoid or eliminate by changing those in the world around us. It was something we were going to have to live with and cope with as needed. For my son, I noticed as elementary school progressed that he came to me less and less to complain about racist incidents. It seemed to me either the incidents weren't occurring, he was coping with them himself, or he was feeling there was nothing he could do about them.

I didn't think it was likely the incidents had stopped. Sometimes David would still share, and we would try to talk to the school or the other kid's parents following the chain of command at the school, trying to make a difference, talking to well-meaning Euro-Americans who could not understand the problem. Most often I would only hear about it later, after David had handled an incident himself.

I wasn't sure how he was managing, until my Korean-born daughter came home in tears. A little girl in her third grade class was coming up and calling her "flat face" every time the teacher wasn't looking. I saw this happen when I helped in the classroom. While driving my kids home from school, we talked about what to do. I asked my son how he would suggest his sister deal with the problem.

David said, "Diana, you have to push her, not too hard, but hard enough. Don't get caught."

Diana said, "I can't fight anybody!"

David replied, "I can't beat up a little girl for you. Well, maybe I could tell her I would."

And so, my son found the little girl alone at recess and told her, "You stop insulting my sister, or I will have to beat you up."

As a parent this went against all the problem solving techniques I had taught my children. But it is what my kids did, and the results were amazing. All the teasing stopped immediately. We didn't have to confront parents, who would have had to feel defensive and explain that no one in their family would ever be racist. We didn't have to confront the teacher and make her feel bad about her classroom management. Was it the "right" way to handle the problem? Would it work for someone else? It certainly might not work and might escalate the problem. I don't advocate this as a way to cope with such incidents among children, only to share our experience. The fact is it worked at a moment in time for David and Diana in the real world. As David says, "At some point you have to stand up for yourself."

By high school David had grown to be five feet eleven inches, taller than most of his Asian American male friends. He was in a basketball game at school with one of his Asian friends, who did not share David's height advantage, and also several Caucasian kids. One of the Euro-American kids, who happened to be shorter than David, made some disparaging remarks about David's Asian friend's ability to play in the game due to his ethnicity. David went over to this kid, looked down at him and asked, "Do you have a problem with Asians?" This Caucasian kid quickly reassured David there was no problem.

Asian Americans Address Racism

Over the years my children discovered they had to stand up for themselves. This was occurring as we were strengthening our family's Asian and Korean American connections. Really being connected as friends and associates was important because it built a level of trust where honest exchanges of information in more depth could occur. As I showed a genuine interest in learning about Koreans and Korean Americans and gathered other adoptive families together, Korean Americans began to become interested in knowing me and my family.

Knowing three particular Korean Americans reinforced what I had begun to understand about political power. In those cases where standing up to racism is beyond the power of an individual, Asian Americans will be there to support each other. I learned the story of Chol Soo Lee from three prominent Korean Americans living near me. Luke and Grace Kim, and K.W. Lee, came together with others to help Chol Soo Lee, who was caught in a current of ignorance and institutionalized racism when he didn't have the voice to protest.

Luke Kim immigrated to the United States in 1956. He had completed medical school and came to the United States to study psychiatry. He became the first Korean to receive a degree in clinical psychology in the United States and was the founding president in 1979 of the National Association of Korean American Psychiatrists. He held positions with the California Department of Corrections and UC Davis Medical Center. He married his wife Grace in 1962, when she immigrated to join him. She earned her master's degree in educational psychology and was a teacher at Davis High School for many years.

K. W. Lee arrived in the United States in 1950. He studied Journalism at West Virginia University and the University of Illinois, becoming the first Asian American journalist to work for mainstream newspapers. He was working as a journalist in the south in the early 1960s covering the African American struggle

K.W. Lee, Grace Kim and Dr. Luke Kim at a Korean American Community Function in spring 2005

for civil rights. He is today known as the "dean of Asian American journalism" and has mentored numerous second-generation Asian American journalists.

Chol Soo Lee did not have an easy start in life. He was born to his mother out of wedlock in Korea. His mother eventually married an American soldier and immigrated to the United States. In 1964, her twelve-year-old son joined her in the United States. Because of his difficulty in learning English, Chol Soo struggled and was teased at school. His mother's marriage was also in trouble. Eventually she divorced. From then on she was working most of the time. With few resources, Chol Soo did not adapt well and ended up in juvenile hall and eventually Napa State Hospital, where he was misdiagnosed as being schizophrenic. In 1973, at age twenty, he was charged with killing a member of the Wah Ching gang in San Francisco's Chinatown. Because of a change of venue, the trial took place in Sacramento. Though there were questions about the court proceedings, Chol Soo was found guilty of first degree murder and was awaiting the gas chamber on San Quentin's death row.

Chol Soo had been on death row for ten years when K.W. Lee heard about the case and began an investigation as a Sacramento Union reporter.

K.W. Lee became convinced Chol Soo Lee was not guilty of the murder. K.W. Lee felt Chol Soo was convicted on the basis of "mistaken identity—all Asians look alike syndrome." Though the murder took place on a crowded street in Chinatown, the only witnesses willing to talk were three Euro-American tourists. Chol Soo Lee was Korean American and the murder was the result of clashes between Chinese gangs, which is one reason the local Asian witnesses were afraid to talk.

The Pan Asian movement to free Chol Soo Lee, that began in the living room of Luke and Grace Kim, ended up connecting not only Korean Americans, but Asian Americans generally across the United States. This led to the retrial and eventual acquittal of Chol Soo Lee. Interestingly, the story is told in the film, *True Believer*, which focuses on the Euro-American attorney in the case, rather than the Asian American movement that produced enough political pressure and raised enough money for the defense to be effective. Chol Soo Lee came from a disadvantaged background, yet Asians of all backgrounds came together to work on his behalf. What the Chol Soo Lee movement tells us is when mass action is needed, Asian Americans will pull together. It can be a comfort to adoptees and adoptive families that they already have a source of support in our children's ethnic communities.

Having Asian American Connections as Armor

Despite having Asian American connections, there still is no template for avoiding racism in the world. While individuals can have group support in egregious circumstances, most of the time adoptees rely on their own coping skills. These will be skills they develop one way or another, either with or without the support of adoptive parents. For the good of my long-term relationships with my children, as a parent I wanted to be able to offer effective support. In middle school my son found racism worse than what he had faced in elementary school. One teacher put a triangular bowl on his head and danced around like a "Chinaman." Another teacher, commenting on the kids' penmanship, told his students he wanted them to write "English," not "Chinese." Whenever my son relayed these incidents, I always wanted to do something.

As David was getting out of the car after I drove him to school one day, I said, "Why don't I talk to the principal?"

His answer was, "Don't make me do it your way! If you do, I am not going to tell you what happens!"

I talked to an adult adoptee friend about it. She said, "It is up to him to choose which battles he wants to fight. Don't make him a cause."

Despite my impulse, by the time my children were in middle school, the battles were not mine to fight. One day David told me of another incident also involving a teacher. It was a science teacher who brought in a sheet of *kim* (seaweed wrapping for sushi). He told the kids it was seaweed, and in Japan they eat it. He offered to let the kids taste it, breaking off little bits and handing it to them. Many promptly spit it in the garbage can. "OOOh yuck!" They said.

When my son told me of this I had much difficulty keeping my temper, but I listened to the rest of what he said. "If the teacher had given them raw potatoes, they would have spit that out too," he said. "You have to put oil and salt on *kim*." It slowly dawned on me this was what Karen had meant when after the multicultural day, she had told me to give my kids armor. Because my son knew Korean Americans, he knew what *kim* was and how one should eat it.

Soon my daughter was attending the same middle school. One day she came home from school and told me she wanted to take Korean food for lunch the next day. She said a boy had brought Korean food that day for lunch. Kids had made some remarks about his "different" food. Diana had said, "I'll eat it with you." She told me his name was Michael Lee, and he had asked her to join a group of kids to fight racism together if something happened to any one of them. She named off some other kids of color in her school who wanted to join the group. Diana told him she would join the group as long as she could still have her white friends, too. She definitely wanted to make Korean food for the next day's lunch. I had a daughter involved in coalition building.

My Own Journey

I began to be in many situations where I was the only non-Asian person. Being in this position I began to learn more about the Asian American experience. The interesting thing is I also began to realize I myself had a cultural heritage. It was an evolutionary process discovering what it means for me personally to be a member of the dominant ethnic group in the United States. I wasn't sure exactly how to handle feelings that came from these experiences. Euro-Americans also need to have pride in who they are.

In Friends of Korea we had discussion groups. We watched movies such as *The Color of Fear*. At one of these discussions a Euro-American man asked a good question, "Why it is okay for every ethnicity except whites to have an exclusive group. If there is a whites only group it is racist," he said. "Why are groups for all these other ethnicities not racist as well?"

I like the answer provided by a Korean American, "Whites being in the majority don't feel the need to organize such groups unless it is for the purpose of suppressing another group. As the majority, their well-being, civil rights, and sometimes even their lives, are not threatened. Think about it. Would there be a group for Koreans in Korea? No, they are the majority there, but Filipino workers in Korea may need such a group. Whites do not need advocacy groups to advocate for their rights within the majority because they are the majority." The answer made good sense to me.

It did not, however, make me feel better about the unease and sense of guilt I sometimes felt for being Euro-American—a member of the majority. It did not help because I knew there ought to be things about my cultural heritage of which I could be proud. I couldn't figure out the balance. I thought of a class I had taken as a freshman in college. It was called "The American Experience," a combination of freshman English, American history, and government. This was a required course for every entering freshman at the University of Texas. It seemed to me to be nothing, but endless bloody films about the murder of innocent people of color by whites. The idea was that in our previous education through high school we would not have been made aware of the harsher elements of the American experience for those who were not Euro-American. Certainly that was true, and I was meant to feel unsettled.

I could never resolve this sense of unease as a university student. Making one feel anxious without resolution is not productive. I continued to feel troubled because there was never any direction on how to be a positive and productive member of the dominant ethnic group. Certainly I did not want to mistreat persons of color. How was I supposed to resolve my feelings of having come from a murderous ancestry? It was complex, because as a child I was told I was English, Irish, Scottish, Swedish, and Welsh. I know just a little about the immigration history of the Irish in America and their struggle against those of English ancestry. Yet it doesn't seem to mean much to me psychologically to be both English and Irish. Before my grandmother died, she confirmed to my mother that we were also German. She had never told my mother because she didn't want my mother, having lived through World War II, to be ashamed of her ancestry. This was an interesting way to manage it. What was lacking in my freshman course was the resolution—how to recognize majority privilege and American history and yet to act appropriately while developing a positive ethnic image.

Lacking in this understanding myself, I was not prepared to offer support to my Euro-American son in developing his self-image either. It is not only Korean-born children who need support around these issues. Because of how long it took me to understand my own ethnicity and cultural heritage, my Caucasian son didn't get much support in that regard when Koreanness entered our family. Luckily he is capable of learning much on his own.

As I found ways for my Korean-born children to become comfortable in connecting with Asian Americans, I noticed they quickly found their own Asian peers and began to find their own mentors. They were working on their task of discovering what it means to be Asian American. It was, after all, their task and not mine. Yet, because they were not adults and I was their parent, it was my responsibility to provide support. As the years went on, I came to realize that in order to be of the most help to them, I had to complete my own task of learning what it means to be white in America, which was my task and not theirs.

The world is not an equal place. Asian adoptees have to find positive things about being Asian, while confronting and dissipating the inferior feelings racism can give rise to. My task is different. I have to realize that as a Euro-American I also have a cultural heritage. For my own self-esteem, I need to feel positive about my ethnicity, recognizing the privileges that arise from being of the dominant ethnicity, without feeling guilt, superiority, or arrogance.

Majority Privilege

Being in the majority confers advantages and protections. The policeman, who is likely also to be Euro-American, is less likely to stop me. I can easily find greeting cards with people who look like me on them. I can take my Americanness for granted. The stores sell clothing in my size. My teachers are likely to be of my ethnicity and share my educational and cultural background. Makeup will be available in my skin tones. I speak English well. My cultural heritage is called "mainstream" and is represented in all the U.S. history books, while the history of Americans of other ethnicities may not be found there. No one questions whether or not I am an American. Majority privilege is a web of institutional and cultural protections for those who look like me. One positive result of my majority privilege may be my conviction that if something is unjust, it can be changed. This can give me courage and confidence. One negative result is that I may not see the world as it really is. I can feel guilt by association even if I personally do not engage in offensive actions. When we feel guilty we may act inappropriately and defensively. Even when I realize I have it, I just may not want to give up my majority privilege. Yet, we have a multiethnic country. In California, Euro-Americans are not the majority anymore.

"White Men's Studies"

I wonder if Euro-Americans can be effective parents for Asian children when we as Caucasian parents don't know who we are. Perhaps in many ways it makes us ineffective parents for Caucasian children as well. I am Euro-American, and I cannot be anything else. Alexis has graduated from college. In order to graduate, he was required to complete a course in any of the various ethnic studies or women's studies. He was lamenting, "Why isn't there a course in white men's studies? That is what I have to figure out how to be."

"You are right, Alexis. That is what we need." It would not be a course for whites only, just as the various other ethnic and women's studies are open to everyone. Not sharing in the majority privilege of whites in America, people of color sometimes may have more understanding of what it means to be white in America than Caucasians do. Hearing their experience is helpful to those who are Euro-American.

Recently I was shopping with a Korean American who made a purchase that would have to be picked up later. The salesman who had learned just a little bit about Korea was trying to greet my friend, saying thank you in Korean, sometimes confusing it with Japanese, and just generally making an idiot out of himself. The salesman probably thought he was being open and friendly; perhaps he couldn't see he was acting superior and condescending.

He definitely could have benefited from "white men's studies." "White men's studies" do exist; it is known as diversity training. Wouldn't it be wonderful if such a course were part of the pre-adoption process for every family adopting interethnically. It would be powerful if it were also part of the training expected of agency social workers. Remembering my son's second grade teacher had training as a multicultural mentor, I find it easy to see one course is not enough, but at least it is a beginning.

Figuring out what ethnic differences mean is a challenge to interethnic adoptive families. On the one hand, the ethnic differences in families mean nothing. In loving each other, the fact some members of a family are Caucasian while others are Asian, is just one facet of who they are collectively. On the other hand, if it is not understood Korean adoptees are having an Asian American experience different from that of Euro-American parents and Caucasian siblings, the ethnic difference can be a gulf too wide to cross. The challenge arises because adoptive parents are handicapped in their perspective when it comes to understanding and supporting the life experience of people of color. This is not the fault of adoptive parents.

Because those in the white majority were raised within Euro-American culture, they swim in the water of underlying cultural assumptions they have been exposed to all their lives. There is no need for them to try to be colorblind or feel defensive just because they don't know what they cannot be expected to know. For the greater good of interethnic relationships within a family, Euro-Americans within that family need to come to understand the privileges their ethnicity brings to them in the United States. If a Euro-American has never taken a course in diversity training, it would be wise to do it.

Choose as Diverse an Environment as Possible

Of course, if like the Staleys, the adoptive family mentioned earlier headed by a Chinese American mother and Euro-American father, interethnic families choose to live with as much diversity as possible, their support system will be built in. It is all a matter of degree. Sarah Park, the second-generation Korean American daughter of one the teachers of our Friends of Korea Kids Club, who is two years older than David, described growing up in the town adjacent to El Dorado Hills where my family lives.

When Sarah Park was six years old, her parents moved from their house in West Sacramento to what Sarah described as "a desolate suburban house in Folsom, California." This became her new home, where she went to school, and where she spent her childhood and adolescent years. To get a sense of the makeup of her new community, one must know Sarah's family had moved into a middle to upper middle class city predominantly populated by Euro-Americans. According to Sarah, "Folsom had a few representatives of minority groups and lower middle class households, but the city overall was representative of white conservative America." Sarah's family was one of a few Asian families who settled in that area during the late 1980s and early 1990s. Wherever her family went, they could be spotted in a crowd because they physically stood out. They did not have the blond-brown hair and light-colored eyes of the majority of the city.

Sarah's personal experience with racism came mostly from school. "For much of my elementary school years, it was not abnormal for me to be one of a few minority children in a classroom," she said. When Sarah says "minority," she is including those from other ethnic groups such as African Americans, Hispanics, and Asians from countries other than Korea. Sarah noted, "Even among Asians I was in the minority back then. When people asked me what ethnicity I was and I replied Korean, they responded that they had never heard of that country before."

Sarah remembered being frustrated and confused about being different from the majority at her school when she was young. She didn't know how to question racist incidents that occurred, and at times felt a little ashamed and embarrassed to bring up the topic. She definitely didn't want to talk to her Euro-American teachers and peers about it, and she didn't know how to effectively address it with her parents. Sarah said, "When I finally did talk to my parents about feeling different, my parents always told me, 'Sarah is Sarah and no one else.'" Sarah's parents consistently emphasized the importance of standing her ground and that helped as she was facing identity and ethnicity issues.

Though she doesn't like to admit it, there were many times in middle and high school when Sarah wished she wasn't Korean. It's not that she was ashamed of her ethnic culture and history, and it wasn't that she wanted to be another ethnicity. She just wanted to be like everyone else and fit in better. There were many times she wished an influx of minorities would come into the city bringing diversity. Though she never verbally expressed it, she hated being one of the few Asian students in class. In a typical classroom of thirty students, she was one of two or three students who were not Caucasian. Sarah speculated, "Perhaps because I was a girl, I wasn't teased as much, but I witnessed other Asian boys being teased and picked on by their Caucasian peers. The white students would tease Asians because we ate different foods, our parents spoke English with an accent, and because we physically looked different with our 'yellow skin' and 'chinky eyes.'" According to Sarah, Asians were called racial slang terms such as "chink" and "gook," and it was not uncommon for white boys to be caught saying "ching chong china man" when they referred to their Asian peers."

Sarah Park in high school.

Despite the bouts with racism I have shared in this book about David at school, it was a shock for me to relate to what

Sarah was saying. When my children were growing up, I felt we were living in an area where we had access to friendships with people of color. After all, I could find Karen in the parking lot at my children's school. My children were never the only person of color in their classroom and certainly not in their grade or their school. There were, however, only one or two Asians teachers over all their school years and no school administrators of color. We were living in California, in a suburb of Sacramento. It has changed a bit. Today there is a Korean church in our town of El Dorado Hills. But, David says Sarah Park gives a good description of the school environment he remembers, with the caveat that El Dorado Hills is one town further away from the diversity of Sacramento, and so a little worse. What I now realize is when I looked at the children in the school and saw ten percent were children of color, I saw diversity. When David and Sarah looked at the children in their schools and saw ninety percent of the children were Euro-American, they felt alone. Because of where we lived, we had some resources, but we could have chosen more diversity.

Giving Adoptees Armor

Many adoptive families live in communities across this country with less diversity than El Dorado Hills had fifteen years ago. In those cases there are inherently more challenges. Many intercountry adoptive families turn to picture books written for the adoption community with examples of what children can do to learn how to handle racist incidents. They might also read books themselves for understanding. It helps if they can go further. Books are only one resource.

Another thing Euro-American adoptive parents tend to do is to go into their children's classrooms and share information about Korea and Asia. Though I do not discourage anyone from going into children's classrooms, and it is good to be involved with your child's school in any case, if one lives in an area lacking in diversity, they are not going to substantially change the school environment by doing this. Racism will still exist. If families of children of color do not live in an area with ethnic diversity, their jobs will be harder. They will have to find a way to strengthen their children from within or, as Karen said, to give them armor. It is likely to be difficult.

Because parents love their children, they want to protect them. Yet, when parents have come to understand subtle, as well as overt, racism, including majority privilege, Euro-American parents can find themselves in a trap. On the one hand, they need to model for their children how to handle racist incidents and how to be proud of being who they are. On the other hand, it is racist in itself for a Caucasian person to tell any person of color how they should manage racism or how they should feel about their ethnicity. If adoptive parents of Asian children want to support their children, the only way out of the trap is to have Asian friends who can be mentors to their children.

Interacting with Asians, learning about their life experiences from the moment Asian children arrive in interethnic-adoptive families, if not before, is important in taking on the future challenges they are going to face. The good news is folks like Karen and Sarah Park's family are living in all the corners of our land. Interethnic adoptive families can find them and befriend them. If Euro-American adoptive parents do not do this, adoptees may wonder, "If my parents have a high regard for Asians, how come they aren't friends with them." If Korean Americans continue to feel foreign to Euro-Americans, what are does this say about their Americanness? There may be times when adoptees want to avoid having Asian friends, to avoid sticking out. Adoptive parents can keep the connection with Asian friends themselves. Those friendships will be needed later.

While Euro-American adoptive parents can immerse themselves in learning about what it means to be Korean, they cannot become Asian any more than their kids can become white. Given the guilt associated with being a member of the majority ethnic group, adoptive parents may wish to avoid being white, just as adoptees can sometimes wish to be white, given this ethnicity difference is a boundary separating family members. Becoming an extended part of the Asian American community, which I believe is a good thing for an adoptive parent to do, is not the same thing as becoming Asian American, any more than becoming an adopted child in a Caucasian family confers "whiteness."

Asians Know Their Own Feelings

Despite the need to step out of oneself and try to understand the adoptee's experience, being an effective parent remains complex. My Euro-American friend's adult Korean-born daughter had an experience that turned out to be meaningful for both my friend and me. Maggie's daughter, Jen, is studying to be a cosmetologist. She lives in a rural area in upstate New York primarily populated by Caucasians.

Recently the cosmetology school held an open house and Maggie attended in support of her daughter. The students had dressed themselves and each other in all sorts of different costumes with fancy hairstyles and makeup. Jen was the only Asian student. Her friends had helped her to dress in a Chinese-style dress with Japanese-style geisha makeup. Maggie and I were shocked at the picture of all the students with Jen appearing as a caricature of an Asian girl, and we wanted to confront what we saw as underlying racism. I called a Korean American friend to discuss what was happening, talking about how we could support Jen in learning to apply makeup in a way that enhanced rather than made a mockery of her Korean features.

My friend caught me off guard. "Was Jen forced to dress like that?"

"No that is the sad part, she seemed to like it," I said.

"The way you are thinking is inherently racist," my friend said. "Who are you to tell Jen how, as an Asian, she should wear makeup?"

Meanwhile, Maggie was talking with adult adoptee, Mark Hagland, who also seemed less than scandalized. He said, "If Jen really wasn't bothered by it, then at least it wasn't a traumatic or harmful situation for her. Different people have different levels of awareness and needs. She is an adult, so it is appropriate for her to choose her responses."

I decided to ask Diana. "Look at this picture," I said, "and tell me what you see."

"They are having a costume party," she said.

"What about the Asian girl?" I asked.

"She looks happy," Diana said.

I asked Diana if that was all she saw. She said, "Oh, I see they forced her to look like that?"

"No, she wanted to," I said.

Diana said, "Well, so what then if she is happy, how is it your problem?"

I was stymied. I called David to look at the picture.

"What do you see?" I asked.

"You'd have to tell me more about it," he said.

Jennifer Dunham at a party with friends from her cosmetology class in spring 2005.

"There is one Asian girl dressed up by her Caucasian friends," I said.

"Well, to me its not a great outfit," he said. "On the other hand I wouldn't judge her. Everyone has to decide for themselves how they want to handle this stuff."

In support of our greater understanding, Jen explained it to Maggie this way. "About a month ago the girls were talking about what they were going to be for the costume party. I said something like, 'What can I be? Maybe I should be an Asian girl.' I was kidding around with ideas around that theme. I have been studying cosmetology with these girls eight hours a day, and they are like family. Had this happened at the beginning when I didn't know them so well, I would have been very uncomfortable. At this point these girls know me as Jen, an individual. It was my idea not theirs. They don't see me as just 'the Asian girl' but as myself. I am accepted. They have never hurt me or disrespected me, so I felt very comfortable playing around with my racial identity. I feel my overall identity is much closer to this group of girls than to others of my own race."

Jen feels that, other than the way she looks and her love for Asian food, she is no more Asian than those white girls. She doesn't know about geisha girls or mandarin Chinese outfits anymore than they do. She has been in many situations where she was uncomfortable and felt badly because of comments about her ethnicity, but this was not one of them.

"So how is this situation different than when you were singing the *Lady and The Tramp* song in second grade?" I asked David.

"The difference is she was not forced and in how she feels about it," David answered. "Racism is there all the time. Each person chooses how and when to deal with it. I deal with it when it is impacting me, when to me it is in my face."

"Do you think anyone who is Caucasian can understand it?"

"I think you understand it, Mom. Mostly you just have to be a good listener."

"So are you glad I made you learn about Korea?" I asked.

"Absolutely," he said. "It has helped me to know who I am."

"Would you dress up in a kung fu outfit?"

"Personally, I wouldn't. I would feel trying to show I am comfortable teasing myself, would itself show I am not comfortable with who I am."

Korean-born adoptees may end up resolving their ethnic identity in a myriad of ways, because of both their environment and who they are as individuals. That is their right. Adoptees are Korean American, not me. I am Euro-American. Being in the majority is my experience. Because my children came to me as children, and not as adults, they needed my help. That was my dilemma. How does someone who is Caucasian, help someone who is Asian to develop their ethnic identity? Euro-Americans cannot usurp an Asian American identity and tell Asians of any age who to be. When parents in an interethnic adoption give their adopted children access to same-race role models, parents help children to work out the puzzle of identity.

Kristi Yamaguchi

In the spring of 1992, I published the following in the *Hand In Hand Newsletter*. Hand In Hand is an adoption support group in the Sacramento area. Here is my short article.

Thank You Kristi Yamaguchi!

We, like so many other families here in Sacramento, enjoyed the winter Olympics. The kids drifted in and out of the room, but my husband, Mark, and I watched a lot of it. My favorite was the skating. Of course I have always enjoyed events that promote international harmony and ethnic diversity, but this year was special. This year for the first time since Dorothy Hamil, an American won the Gold in women's figure skating.

My son, David, was watching the final evening with me, not terribly interested. I explained these were the best skaters in the whole world, and one of them was going to win a prize. Being pretty competitive, he decided to watch as the American began to skate.

His comment was, "I thought she was American, why does she have brown hair?"

"Well David," I replied, "I told you Americans come from everywhere."

He looked skeptical then intrigued as she not only won, but stood proudly singing the American song as they raised the American flag. Now David hates my examples and lectures. He pretty much thinks I'm always trying to run things. But, my little American of Korean ancestry decided his mother couldn't have staged an event this big and gotten the news media to cover it. Though my husband Mark says he wouldn't put it past me. David has been an American only a very short time. He is nearly eight and arrived home just two years ago. He still struggles with English and hates being different.

I was so pleased when he smiled and said, "Kristi's an American like me!"

Racism Is There Whether You Like It or Not

In the thirteen years since I wrote the "Thank you Kristi Yamaguchi!" article, I have changed a lot. Growing as an adoptive parent is as much a developmental process as it is for an adoptee. My perspective has changed. I know growing and changing will be a part of my life into the future. At the time I wrote the article, I knew my son's sense of being fully American was challenged by the racism he had already begun to face. When I started to understand he was having a different adoption experience than I was having, I believed if I gave him the right examples and role models, we could avoid racism. At the time, I didn't realize this might be an arrogant assumption, coming from my own cultural background and perspective as a Euro-American. I didn't understand racism is not something that people of color avoid, but something they cope with. Being a member of the white majority had not given me the tools to solve my son's life challenges. If I hadn't been white, I couldn't have solved them either, as each individual's life belongs only to them. But I would have been better equipped to offer support. In writing the "Thank you Kristi Yamguchi!" article I was so happy to be tying everything into a nice package for my son.

It was not wrong to point out Asian Americans, like Kristi Yamaguchi, were accomplishing many things. Such an understanding can give adoptees a sense of pride. What was wrong was to assume that because of Kristi Yamaguchi's accomplishment, racism against Asians had ceased to exist or had become trivial. I was hoping if David knew about Kristi Yamaguchi, saw the world the way I saw it, my perspective would become his perspective. It doesn't work that way. I was to learn that was not enough. It takes so much more. I needed to try to see the world the way my children saw it.

What I have learned over the years is racism faced by Asian children is not something that can be eliminated or avoided by parents, no matter what they do. I spent years taking Korean treats to school parties, teaching kids in my children's school classes about Korean drums and hanboks, hoping to enlighten teachers and children at school to make it a more pleasant life space for my kids. Those experiences were positive and perhaps somewhat helpful. On the whole, I think it was like dropping pebbles into a well. It would take way too many to fill it up. The world around us remained pretty much the same—racism subtle and sometimes blatant were part of our lives.

When I wrote the "Thank you Kristi Yamaguchi!" article, I had not yet seen the reporting on figure skater Michelle Kwan in the 2000 Olympics. Favored to win, Chinese American Michelle Kwan was beaten by Euro-American Sarah Hughes, who skated the performance of a lifetime. The headline in the *Seattle Times* read, "Hughes as good as gold, American outshines Kwan." The implication was Michelle Kwan was not American. Incidents such as these have left me to understand that within this country some are seen as more American than others. Note the reporting on Michelle Kwan occurred in Seattle, which boasts a significant Asian American population and Asian American political leaders.

Are Michelle Kwan and Kristi Yamaguchi only American when there is no one blue-eyed and blonde-haired around to serve as a representative? My son could see he was on the edge of Americanness when he was only eight, but he had to wait for me to grow up for me to see it. Over the years David has continued to let me know his acceptance as an American is often challenged. It is not a problem I can fix. It is arrogant to think I can. The multicultural, multiethnic challenges of America run deeper than that. Euro-Americans are not the leaders in determining the needs of Asian American communities or the ethnic needs of their own children. This thing called ethnicity in my family can mean nothing in determining the depth of love we share with each other, or it can become very big, depending on how we define the boundaries. Euro-American adoptive parents cannot prevent either blatant or subtle racism their children have to face as Asian Americans, despite their best intentions and efforts, even in places with the diversity of California.

It is so much harder for both me and my children when I don't reach out. Because I have Asians, Korean Americans, Adoptees, Asian adoptive parents and fellow Euro-American adoptive parents as friends, I continue to learn so much. I can have meaningful discussions and feel supported in the complexity of this life experience.

Building a Network

백짓장도 맞들면 낫다

Even a sheet of paper seems lighter when two people lift it together.
KOREAN PROVERB

Isolation

Prior to the mid 1990s, most adoptees from Korea lived their lives isolated from other Korean Americans and from one another. Adult adoptees spoke about what the experience of isolation was like at the leadership conference at which the Korean American Adoptee Adoptive Family Network was born. "I felt a sense of isolation from other Korean Americans throughout my life," said one adoptee. Though living in California, he said he felt he had been walking through life along a wall. He was on one side and Korean Americans were on the other side. Sometimes there had been a window in the wall. During these times, he could see Korean Americans and they could see him, but they couldn't communicate. He said sometimes he wanted to make funny faces at the window to see if there was a reaction. He said he craved communication and dialogue.

Another adoptee from Canada also spoke. He was talking about his isolation, not only from Korean Canadians, but also from other Korean adoptees. After being raised on a farm in Canada, he told how he had managed to "infiltrate" the Korean Community in Toronto in his young adulthood. Since that time he had also managed a trip to Korea looking for birth family.

He talked of going to his adoption agency in Korea. He was asked to register in a book and noticed a few pages with the names of other adoptees who had visited the agency. Not having known any fellow adoptees, and seeing the pages with the names and addresses of several, he asked the social worker if he could photocopy the pages. She told him he couldn't, but while she went to get his records he began scribbling names and addresses frantically into a comic book he was carrying. Later on the subway, he lost most of the addresses he was carrying, but he still had one. One day he decided to make a phone call using the contact information he had retained for one fellow Korean adoptee.

"Hello, is L there?"

"This is L."

"Hi, I am from Toronto, Canada. I came from the same adoption agency in Korea as you did."

"No way!" she said.

This story showed the amount of excitement adoptees felt connecting with another adoptee when they had been in isolation. A self-supporting student, this adoptee had managed to get himself to Sacramento for our leadership conference to have this chance to be with others like himself and have his voice heard. I was privileged to have had some role in building a network that took adoptees and adoptive families away from that era of isolation.

The 1988 Seoul Olympics

Though I didn't know it, from the beginning of my adoption experience, I was part of a movement that would connect adoptees and adoptive families with a sense of community. My husband and I adopted our children at a remarkable time relative to Korean adoption history. When we first began our exploration of adoption as the means of enlarging our family, we were not aware adoption from Korea was still occurring. We ended up adopting from Korea when it became our best and most comfortable option. What is most interesting is that during this time when we were unaware of adoption from Korea, average Koreans and Korean Americans were mostly unaware of it as well. Certainly they were unaware of the scope of it.

When we traveled to Korea to pick up our daughter in March 1988, preparations for the Olympics were well underway. Many of the buildings were wrapped in tarps in the process of renovation. We stayed at the Seoul YMCA hotel on Chongno. One day while we were out sightseeing, they wallpapered the room we were staying in. The Olympic mascot, Hodori (a tiger in a *samulnori* hat), was everywhere, as were Seoul Olympics T-shirts. We bought a T-shirt for each of us, my husband, my son, and our soon-to-be daughter in anticipation of watching Korea on TV when we got home. We were excited that soon the whole world was going to see what we had just discovered, Korea, a blooming bustling country grown out of the dust of war.

A few months after we returned home with Diana, we sat down to watch every bit of Olympic coverage we could find. Along with short clips about *hanboks*, *kimchi*, *ginseng*, and Korean architecture as different from that of China or Japan, there were those on Korea's rapid industrialization and its "export of babies." More children were leaving for adoption to other countries per year than ever before. Journalists covering the Olympics went indepth on the story of Korean adoption and why it was occurring, embarrassing the Korean government.

During the first forty years of Korean adoption to the United States the experience was, for many, one of isolation. There was no Internet or national support network to connect adoptees and adoptive families. There was no visible Korean adoption community. In some areas adoption support groups existed. There were some magazines and conferences, but they did not reach most adoptive families. In some areas forward-thinking individuals did develop programs for Korean adoptees and their families. East Rock Institute welcomed adoptive families from as early as 1973 to their

Alexis, Diana, Chris, and Mark watch the 1988 Seoul Olympics.

Korean American conference, which led to a number of other programs. The Korean Institute of Minnesota, a Saturday Korean School program, began operating in 1975. Korean adopted adult, Deborah Johnson MSW, one of our invited speakers, began involvement with Korean adoptees and adoptive families in a professional way in 1983. The programs that did exist were disconnected from each other. People in different parts of the United States struggled to develop similar programs as though each program was the first of its kind, repeating similar mistakes and not building on the efforts of others. Programs focused on the needs of adult adoptees were virtually nonexistent. Korean adoptees were so scattered, especially in rural areas, that they could graduate from high school without ever seeing another Asian American.

Though the isolation still continued for most in the adoption community, which could hardly be called a "community" then, I believe the beginnings of our opportunities for connecting began with the Seoul Olympics. For better or worse, and I believe it was for the better, Korean adoptees and their families became more visible to each other, to Korean Americans, and to Koreans. Those Olympics provided the spark that set enough people on fire that efforts at building community became inevitable.

Community Building Through Friends of Korea

In an earlier chapter, I described the steps we took here in Sacramento toward connecting with the local Korean American community. A core group of adoptive families made efforts to enter the Korean American Community through the Korean School of Sacramento, the results of which led to the formation of Friends of Korea. We were our own laboratory, only marginally aware of the efforts of others in other places. The Internet eventually made it possible for people to build a more connected Korean adoption community, but many people worked hard to build the network.

Though I was unaware of it at the time, I now know that as I began to reach out to Koreans and Korean Americans in California, adoptees in Europe had begun forming support organization and there were a few adoptees becoming visible in Korea. I mention some here that I am aware of; I know there were others. While our core group of Sacramento families was participating in the pilot program for adoptees through the Korean School of Sacramento in the summer of 1993, Mihee Nathalie Lemoine, adopted from Korea to Belgium, returned to live in Korea. She had searched successfully and had found her birthmother. She then began working to help others who wanted to search for their birth families. She went on to help hundreds of adoptees and birth parents to reconnect. To further support her birth family search efforts, in 1994 Mihee founded an organization called the Euro-Korean League for Korean Overseas Adoptees.

In 1995, just after we had succeeded in incorporating Friends of Korea, Wayne Berry from Minnesota also met and visited his birth family in Korea. In his desire to help other adoptees who wanted to find birth family, he established the Korean Adoption Registry. In the fall of 1995, Korean adoptee Brian Bauman, who was attending the Air Force Academy in Colorado, developed leukemia. A Korean Broadcast Service documentary about his plight and his need for a compatible bone marrow donor aired in

Korea. Early in 1996 Koreans responded in droves to help, and a suitable donor was found.

Adult Adoptees Become Real to Me

When Friends of Korea began its Sacramento Korean adoption community building efforts, I had very limited contact with adult Korean-born adoptees. I knew adult adoptees must exist, of course. I could see my own children growing in that direction every day. I mentioned previously that my husband's close friend while growing up in Corpus Christi, Texas was Jeff Hobbs, whose sister and brother, Jenny and John, were adopted from Korea, but I did not know Jeff's siblings well. It turns out Jenny Hobbs was the child, Yummy, that Harry Holt brought to the United States along with the eight children he adopted from Korea in 1955. It was the beginning of a flood of Korean adoption through Holt Children's Services, the agency Harry Holt founded. Years after we adopted our children, it was a shock to me to see a picture of Jeff Hobbs' family when reading the book, *Seed from the East*, by Bertha Holt which chronicles the Holt Korean adoption legacy. I knew of adult adoptees, but I did not know them as friends. To me they were invisible.

I first met adopted adult, Su Niles, here in Sacramento in 1992 at an adoption agency picnic. When our group of adoptive families moved out of the Korean School of Sacramento and formed Friends of Korea, Su began to attend all of our discussion groups and activities. In July 1996, she expressed the desire for a safe space for adoptees in their own group, specifically for adult adoptees only—a place where they could come and begin to know each other without input or criticism from adoptive parents. When Su decided to form the Sacramento Adult Adoptee Group, Friends of Korea supported her. At the beginning Su found some members of the group herself. I sent out letters to old Hand in Hand support group addresses from twenty years before. We figured those adoptive families now had adult adoptees within them. Many letters came back, as the addresses were no longer good. Most letters landed where they landed, but we found one adult adoptee through this process. By this time, Friends of Korea was sending out a quarterly newsletter to the address of every adoptive family and interested Korean American we could find. The following are excerpts of what Su wrote for the July 1996 issue of the *Friends of Korea Newsletter*:

"Korean Adoptees and the Korean American Community, the two have always seemed to be separate, distinct groups. Through the efforts of Friends of Korea, the two groups are now connecting. It is my hope that as the Sacramento Adult Adoptee Group flourishes, we can have meaningful exchanges of life experiences, culture, and language that will create a unique bond. Please encourage adult adoptees you may come across through your daily lives and who may be searching for a group such as ours to contact me, and they will be most warmly welcome." Su Niles

Su Niles, founder of the Sacramento Korean Adoptee Group.

Adult adoptees did come, and the Sacramento Adult Adoptee Group came into being. They held their own meetings led by adoptees for their mutual support.

Korean Americans and the Korean Government Listen to Friends of Korea

Our Friends of Korea core group attended many Korean American Community events, and our visibility grew. In November 1996, the Korean Consulate in San Francisco asked us to make a presentation for them on the lives and needs of Korean American adoptees. Su Niles and I made the presentation together. Su spoke about the experiences of adult adoptees, and I represented adoptive families. We asked the consulate to give us support in building and expanding our groups.

Also in the fall of 1996, Cynthia Goldberg, a member of our original core group, suggested we attend a conference on Korean American youth at The University of California at Berkeley. After meeting at Cynthia's house, we loaded our Friends of Korea members into my van: adoptive parents, bilingual Korean American immigrants, and a Korean American adoptee. The conference was primarily in Korean, but it was open to anyone who wanted to attend. With our translators we were in some sense crashing their party. We sat under a banner that read "Korean American Youth and Their Ethnic Identity."

Clearly, adopted children fit the category of Korean American Youth, in fact adoptees represent ten percent of Korean immigration, but adoptees had not been included as a component of the conference. This lack of inclusion was mostly because the organizers had not thought to do it, and certainly they wouldn't have known how to do it. They were disconnected from the adoption community and barely knew adoptees and adoptive families existed, but they were receptive to learning about them. At a forum concluding the conference, the adoptee who accompanied us made some well-received, heartfelt statements asking for inclusion in the Korean American community as an adoptee and fellow Korean American.

Chris with Cynthia Goldberg at a Friends of Korea event in February 1997.

Friends of Korea Organizes a Leadership Conference

By early 1997, it was clear that for us to overcome isolation, for there to exist a visible Korean adoption community, even if it spoke with a variety of voices, we needed to be at least loosely connected. Our Korean American Friends of Korea board members, Dr. Eyoungsoo Park, and Dr. Luke Kim and his wife Grace Kim continued making outreaches on behalf of Friends of Korea to the Korean government. They were asking the Korean government to support Friends of Korea in organizing a leadership conference to build a national organization connecting the adoption community across the United States. For the leadership conference to be successful, we felt it should include Koreans, Korean Americans, adoptees, and adoptive families. We felt it should be formed by adoptees and adoptive parents working together, and it should be geographically diverse with representatives in various parts of the United States. Friends of Korea raised the funds to sponsor the conference and pay the airfares and hotel expenses of adoptee and adoptive parent leaders from across the United States to come to the conference. Contributions to the effort were made by the Korean Consulate in San Francisco, the Dry Cleaners Association of Sacramento, and the Northern California Marine Corps Veterans. Since we were in isolation, how could we find the leaders to invite to the leadership conference?

A new magazine for Korean Americans, primarily second-generation who were more comfortable in English, had appeared in 1996. It was called *Woori* or *WE Magazine*. In January 1997 their cover read "American by Adoption: The Lives of Korean American Adoptees." Su Niles and I had both contributed articles. In this magazine, the editors reached out to individuals within the adoption community that they could find. It wasn't a review of all the programs or individuals connected to Korean adoption, but those programs and individuals that were visible to the editors at the magazine. Because Friends of Korea was also in the magazine, and we received a copy, these people and programs became visible to us as well. Those of us in Friends of Korea decided to reach out to adoptees and adoptive parents who were in the magazine to invite them to be speakers for a leadership conference sponsored by Friends of Korea.

Of those adoptees and adoptive parents we invited from the *WE* magazine pieces, Wayne Berry, Deborah Johnson, and Lindy Gelber attended. Though Jo Rankin wasn't able to attend, she sent prepared remarks and Tom Manvydas attended as her representative.

They were all people who had shown leadership. Deborah Johnson, MSW, living in Minnesota was adopted from Korea. She is a social worker and an adoption/diversity consultant and trainer, as well as a nationally recognized expert on adoption issues for internationally adopted children. She has created numerous curriculums for various culture camps and escorts families to Korea with the Korea Ties Program.

As I previously mentioned, Wayne Berry had created the Korean Adoption Registry in Minnesota. Following his own successful search for birth family, he created a video called *Completing My Puzzle*. He wanted to try to help other adoptees to also find resources.

Lindy Gelber founded Camp Sejong located in New Jersey, with an emphasis on the creative arts, just plain fun, and well-known Korean American role models. Some Koreans and Korean Americans who have come to Camp Sejong include LA Dodger pitcher Chan Ho Park, NHL Hockey star Jim Paek, Olympic skater Lilly Lee, adoptee book illustrator Chris Soenpiet, The Ahn trio, and Olympic diver Dr. Sammy Lee. Lindy presented a paper delivered at Yale University to honor The East Rock Institute on the Occasion of its 25th anniversary on October 28, 1995. The paper was called "The Social, Economic, and Political Benefits to The Korean and Adoptive Communities through Unification."

Tom Manvydas MBA was an adult adoptee living near Los Angeles and working for Metagenics Incorporated. Tom was active in the Korean American community in Los Angeles, working on programs for both adopted and second-generation kids. He helped organize an annual Korean culture day and developed a Korean heritage school program.

Jo Rankin was an adult adoptee in Los Angeles. She worked at KCET-TV and was gaining her own visibility. She and Tonya Bishoff were co-editors of the first anthology of writings by adult adoptees, *Seeds from a Silent Tree*. What was amazing to me was not only the torrent of feeling conveying longing and loss from an adult adoptee perspective in the book they assembled, but the fact they were able to do it at all. I was still reaching here and there to connect with adoptees and adoptive families in whatever way I could. Somehow the editors of the anthology found many adoptees, not only willing to share their experiences honestly, but also with the ability to put them into writing. I recently learned their first attempt to find Korean adoptee writers was through *Poets and Writer's Magazine*. With these people in mind as speakers, Friends of Korea began working on the leadership conference that would form KAAN.

Jo Rankin, co-editor of the first anthology of writings by Korean-born adoptees.

Meanwhile, Jo Rankin had become connected with The Global Korean Network (GKN). GKN held their second annual winter conference on February 22-23, 1997. When I contacted Jo in January 1997 about our plans for a leadership conference, she suggested Friends of Korea send an adoptee representative to the GKN Conference as well. We sent the adoptee who had previously attended the Korean American Youth and Their Ethnic Identity Conference to the GKN Conference. When she returned, I interviewed her for the Friends of Korea newsletter. She said, "I assumed it would be another conference, mostly focusing on the needs of immigrant Korean adults and their families. To my surprise, not only were there first and second-generation Korean Americans, and a few non-Koreans, but the majority were Korean adoptees. Heart-filled thank you to GKN for making us feel a part of the Korean community and to Friends of Korea for giving me the opportunity to attend this conference."

As we worked on the plans for the leadership conference, Eyoung-soo and I began thinking of all the ways we could ask for inclusion for adoptees in programs that already existed for Korean Americans in Korea. Eyoungsoo suggested I write a letter to the President of Korea, Kim Young Sam, asking him to include adoptees in the World Korean Ethnic Festival. Eyoungsoo had previously attended the festival and no adoptees had been represented. We were, of course, unaware adoptees, such as Tobias Hübinette from Europe, had broken that barrier. I am not sure where the letter ended up, but at least the consulate in San Francisco was listening. In September 1997, Friends of Korea was asked to recommend three adoptees from Sacramento to attend the festival, which we did.

Also in fall 1997, North Park University in Chicago invited me to their seventh symposium, "Korean Americans: The New American Mosaic." I wondered how to make a presentation that would be well received and understood. After conversations with Eyoungsoo, I knew what to say. On October 11, 1997, I presented a paper "Standing on the Bridge, The Story of Friends of Korea (The Sacramento Model for Korean American Community and Adoptive Family Member Interaction)."

I later learned that in this same time period, in November 1997, four adult adoptee artists held a multimedia art performance in Seoul called "Space for Shadows." The exhibition was sponsored by the Han Diaspora and featured the work of Kate Hers, Miok Song Bruning, Me-K Ahn, and Susan Sponsler. One result of this exhibit was pressure on the Korean government for extended visas for adoptees who wanted to visit their homeland for an extended stay. *Korean Quarterly*, a non-profit, volunteer publication created by and for the Korean American community, which included adopted Koreans and their families in Minnesota also came into being in 1997.

In February 1998, I happened to be traveling to Korea in support of final preparations for the leadership conference. Learning of this, Consul General Ri Hoon Hur at the Korean Consulate in San Francisco asked

Invitation to the inauguration of President Kim Dae Jung.

me if I would like to attend the inauguration of incoming president Kim Dae Jung. If I wanted to do that, he could arrange it. Of course, I wanted to do that.

On February 25, 1998, I was there when the South Korean government made a peaceful transition of power from the ruling to the opposition party, a clear change from dictatorship to democracy. I rode with other foreign dignitaries through flag-lined streets on a shuttle bus from the Hyatt Hotel to the inauguration ceremony, chatting with the daughter of the Philippine Ambassador, a congressman from the Korean district in Los

Angeles, a steel executive from Beijing, and an American East Coast newspaper reporter who had interviewed Kim Dae Jung in jail. I was able to say, when asked my connection to Korea, that I was the adoptive mother of two Korean-born children, a connection I felt was as important as any other.

Chris at the inauguration ceremony of President Kim Dae Jung.

Friends of Korea Hosts the Leadership Conference that Forms KAAN

In April 1998, Friends of Korea burst the bonds of our group's own isolation in Sacramento. The leadership conference in Sacramento, California, arranged and supported by Friends of Korea, was the first of its kind in that it combined Korean government leaders, Korean American leaders, adoptee leaders, and adoptive parent leaders trying to make national connections. Through the video of the leadership conference made by Elaine Williams, one of Friends of Korea's original core group, whose hobby was video editing, I can still reflect on these events that Friends of Korea offered to Korean adoption history.

(From left to right) Dr. Eyoungsoo Park, Tom Manvydas, Su Niles, Deborah Johnson, Wayne Berry, Consul General Ri-Hoon Hur and his wife, Chris Winston, Lindy Gelber, Grace Kim, Luke Kim, Education director Jung Ae Kim, and two consular representatives at the leadership conference.

The leadership conference that formed the Korean American Adoptee Adoptive Network (KAAN) was held on April 18, 1998. We brought those prominent invited leaders from across the United States to speak, and they spoke eloquently. Yet, as a grass roots organization, KAAN has always felt every voice in the adoption community has value. We allowed all adoption community members in attendance at the leadership conference to speak if they wanted to do so, because the network we were forming would belong to all of us connected to Korean adoption.

Korean American Community Support

Eyoungsoo served as moderator of the leadership conference. Always wanting others to be more prominent than himself, he made sure all the

others present had an opportunity to express themselves,
building bridges between the
Korean Americans, Korean government, and a newly emerging
Korean adoption community.
As a psychologist, he was enjoying this opportunity to share
creative ideas and foster growth
in others.

Eyoungsoo has shared many connections. Here he introduces Korean Congressman, Jay Yoo to members of our Friends of Korea Family Exchange Program travel group in summer 1998 following the leadership conference. We enjoyed a tour of the Korean Congress.

Grace Kim spoke at the conference representing the Korean American Community Association of Sacramento. Grace said, "First generation
Korean American immigrants have been busy and preoccupied with their
own survival issues and have been slow in paying attention to the Korean
adoptees in this country. Perhaps Koreans and Korean Americans have
mixed feelings about the Korean children who were adopted out to foreign
countries. They feel very grateful to the adoptive families for taking care
of Korean children, and at the same time, many of them feel guilty and
ashamed about biological Korean parents having to abandon the children.
This is an emotional issue they may want to deny or not think about."

Chris talking with the Korean Ambassador and Luke and Grace Kim at a reception following the 2003 KAAN Conference in Washington D.C. Luke and Grace know everyone.

I know very well the success
of putting together this leadership
conference was because of the supportive friendship I share with Luke
and Grace Kim. It is difficult for a
Euro-American adoptive parent or a
Korean-born adoptee to make connections in Korea without the help
and support of Korean Americans.
Luke and Grace Kim have been ad-
vocates for Friends of Korea, KAAN,
and the adoption community.

Voices of a Sacramento Adoptee and Adoptive Parent

At the leadership conference, adult adoptee, Su Niles, stood to speak, looking striking in a purple suit, her hair cropped short. She was reaching out to the Koreans and Korean Americans who were present. "We want to understand what it is *in* here," Su Niles said, pointing at her heart, "what is *on* here," she continued pointing at her face, "and the only place we can get that understanding is from you. I stand before you as a representative of my Sacramento Adult Adoptee group who does search, not just for their birth parents or their families of origin, but for their culture, for their identities as Koreans, what it means to be Korean, but also taking into consideration we were raised on American soil. We can't go back and change that. How can we meet each other somehow, somewhere in the middle?"

Adoptive parent Cynthia Goldberg wrote in the leadership conference booklet, "As parents we know a lot more about Korea and Korean American life than we used to. This knowledge is part of our lives, as it should be. We don't 'do Korea' once a year. It's here everyday. Our family sends thanks to the generous and welcoming Korean Americans in Sacramento who have stretched themselves to include adoptive families into their small circle. They have enriched our lives and we hope that we have been able to give something back to them in return."

Korean Government Listens

Ri Hoon Hur, Consul General, Korean Consulate San Francisco played an important part in putting together the leadership conference, offering financial and moral support. He recognized our need for community, acknowledging that even a sheet of paper is lighter when two people lift it together. The San Francisco Consulate had encouraged Friends of Korea to focus nationally and internationally, rather than be limited to Sacramento or California. At the leadership conference, Consul General Hur said, "Ladies and Gentlemen, It is a pleasure to address you this afternoon and to be among so many people who deeply care about Korea. I am reminded of the enrichment I receive from gathering together for an evening of good conversations with friends or a family celebration with relatives. I think a sense of community must be a universal need. Everyone needs to share common interests, or a common past, and the comfort of being among the familiar. In this respect, I believe the need for adoptees and adoptive families to form a national group is not only absolute, but long overdue. As the Friends of Korea literature poignantly makes clear, when an adopted child grows up and is suddenly confronted by an identity crisis, it is too late."

At the leadership conference, the Consul General revealed that the new president Kim Dae Jung was very interested in reaching out to adoptees, and he was likely to visit San Francisco in June 1988. We asked Consul General Hur to ask President Kim Dae Jung if the newly formed Korean American Adoptee Adoptive Family Network (KAAN) could present him with a gift upon his visit.

The Consul General replied, "I will certainly recommend that if he ever comes here."

Following the leadership conference, Consul General Hur called me and told me the new Korean president, Kim Dae Jung, was indeed coming. He told me that at the reception at the consulate, two children would be selected to give flowers to Kim Dae Jung and his wife Lee Hee Ho.

"Why don't you choose one eight-year-old adoptee from your Friends of Korea Korean Language and Culture School," Consul General Hur said, "boy or girl doesn't matter. After you let me know who it is, we will choose a child of the other sex from among second generation Korean Americans."

I called to let the Consul General know eight-year-old Kevin Clendenin would be happy to participate and present the flowers. The picture of Kevin presenting the flowers to Kim Dae Jung remains on the KAAN website. We then did as much outreach as we could to groups related to Korean adoption that we could find across the United States. We asked

Kevin Clendenin shakes hands with President Kim Dae Jung on his post inaugural visit to San Francisco.

everyone in the Korean adoption community to send a postcard or picture for us to put in a box to give to President Kim Dae Jung. We were excited when the response was strong enough to fill the box.

Kim Dae Jung wanted to reach out to adoptees further. For "The Feel and Touch Motherland Tour," he invited twenty-nine adoptees, seventeen from the United States and twelve from Europe. Consul General Ri Hoon Hur asked for a recommendation from the Sacramento Adult Adoptee Group and Friends of Korea to fill six of those slots from the United States. Su Niles could not travel because she did not want to leave her dad who had been diagnosed with cancer. Su and I chose six Sacramento adoptees for this trip of a lifetime. The consulate let us know they had also contacted the Korean Consulate in Canada to include the Canadian adoptee who had been so eloquent on the topic of isolation at our leadership conference. During the trip President Kim Dae Jung held a forty-five minute meeting with the adoptees, where he apologized to them for sending them out of Korea for adoption. This is an apology that brought mixed reactions. For some adoptive parents and adoptees, believing in adoption from Korea as the best option for Korean children without families, the apology was offensive. For some adoptees that had experienced hardships as a result of their adoptions, the apology was welcome. However, when adoptions did not stop following this apology, the apology seemed insincere. For some adoptees and adoptive families, the apology was an acknowledgement of the adoptees existence and their continuing value to Korea. For this last group, the apology was appreciated.

Outcome of the Leadership Conference

The outcome of the KAAN leadership conference was that the concept of a national network, rather than a national organization was needed. An important function of the network would be to hold an annual national conference. Deborah Johnson came up with the name for the network, The Korean American Adoptee Adoptive Family Network (KAAN). We all agreed no one wanted to see an umbrella organization over all the local groups telling them how to do their work. Groups were scattered across this country, some long-established, some new, some with names, some without names, some incorporated, some not, some for profit, some not, and all providing various support and services for adoptees and adoptive families. The local groups are all different, each with its own heart and soul developed by those who put it together. The groups might like to share ideas with each other, but the needs and resources in different locations are varied.

It made sense to begin with a language school in Sacramento because those were the resources available to Friends of Korea. In Minnesota, the Korean Institute of Minnesota was also flourishing. However in Michigan, for instance, the resources there made culture camps more reasonable projects. The flavor in Michigan was for a grassroots adoptive parent organized structure for their culture camp. In Colorado the Korean Heritage Camp was one of a more formal series of camps for adoptees from many countries. In some areas groups for adult adoptees had arisen offering social support. The groups were not "one size fits all." KAAN was not planning to tell, and the local organizations weren't going to let KAAN tell them how they should run their local groups. This didn't mean a network wasn't needed. The term network implies an association among equals. For the network to meet the needs of all, it needed to be loose in structure and open and inclusive of all groups related to Korean Adoption, no matter their individual structure or focus.

We all agreed KAAN should accommodate the wide range of opinions within our community and not take positions representing the adoption community, so all voices could be heard. We agreed it was important to become more connected and less isolated. To accomplish those goals, we agreed to work toward holding an annual national conference that encouraged interaction between adult adoptees, younger adoptees, adoptive parents, Koreans, and Korean Americans. The invited speakers who attended the leadership conference became the working committee for the first national KAAN Conference. We had moved out of the era of isolation.

Korean American Adoptee Adoptive Family Network

칼 제 자루 못 깎는다

A kitchen knife cannot carve its own handle.
KOREAN PROVERB

An Annual Summer Event

It happens every summer, my excitement builds as the annual national KAAN conference is fast approaching. Every summer since 1999, I have enjoyed this chance for my family and myself to reconnect with those who share our life experience. It is a chance to renew connections and friendships with adoptive parents, adoptees, Koreans, and Korean Americans, who are "regulars," coming from places all across the United States. It is also a chance to meet new friends who are coming for the first time, both as individuals and as representatives of groups. Not bound by any of the limits of email and virtual connection, this annual coming together allows all attendees to feel part of a national adoption community.

The conference is a moment in time when Koreans, Korean Americans, adoptees, and adoptive families come together to interact with each other. Though the local community hosting the conference has had national support, the conference belongs to the community where it is held. It is their chance to show the vibrancy and uniqueness of their local adoption community to all their visitors. The hosting community will have done significant fundraising and will have helped select proposals as part of the programming committee. One older adult adoptee, one young adult adoptee who is eighteen to twenty-two years old, one adoptive parent, and one Korean American will have shown leadership in pulling their constituencies together for this conference. In many locations the KAAN Conference also derives support from forward thinking adoption agencies.

Nerves may be a bit frazzled from the work it took to put the conference together, but from the opportunity to work together on a national event, the local community will have been strengthened, and the national network will have been extended. All of us who attend will meet adoptees, adoptive parents, Koreans and Korean Americans, some of whom share our views, and some of whom see things quite differently from us. Each voice has value. In their entirety, those voices represent my fellow adoption community members, connected because adoption from Korea is part of our life experience. Whether we agree or disagree, and however we choose to live our lives, at the KAAN conference we come together physically from across this country to reconnect, share, and grow. I remember the first one.

The First KAAN Conference

Following the leadership conference, we proceeded forward to put together the first national conference for adoptees, adoptive families, Koreans and Korean Americans. We felt the conference content ought to recognize the new outreach by Koreans and Korean Americans. We wanted to hold the conference in Los Angeles, the largest Korean American community in the United States. We relished the symbolism of being welcomed there. There were other reasons as well. Ed Chang from U.C. Riverside, who I had met at the Conference on Korean American Youth in Berkeley, was willing to help. Jo Rankin and Tom Manvydas were there. It seemed a good place to start. Tom Manvydas and I were to be the conference co-chairs.

Ed Chang was exceedingly helpful, especially given our naiveté and confusion about what we were doing. He took us to the Radisson on Wilshire Boulevard, which was owned by Korean Americans. Despite our having no previous credit record, Ed's introduction of us gave us the in we needed. Additionally, we were charging a registration fee of eighty dollars per person for adults, forty dollars per person for children, teens, and college students. Since at a hotel the lunch alone can be a minimum of forty dollars, and we were offering breakfast, lunch, and dinner, we were not even covering the food costs. Yet, we were paying for our speakers' hotel rooms and travel expenses from across the country, and from Korea. This is to say nothing of audiovisual costs. Fundraising was an overwhelming task. I remain thankful to Ed Chang for introducing us to so many Korean Americans in Los Angeles who helped us with the conference.

We intended that the conference meet the needs of all participants which included, adopted children of ages eight and up, adult adoptees, adoptive parents, Koreans, and Korean Americans. Immediately adult adoptees on behalf of themselves, and adoptive parents on behalf of younger adoptees began crashing into each other, competing for resources. It was like we had all been wandering around in a desert for forty years and had suddenly found the water of Korea. It seemed like it was limited in supply and worth fighting for. The hard work and sometimes hard feelings of it were tuition well paid. We learned how to delineate our mutual and exclusive needs and how to respect boundaries.

Despite the difficulties, the first national KAAN conference, held July 23-25, 1999, was historic. The theme was "A Tapestry of Voices and Energies Raised in Unity." Korean American youth organizations in Los Angeles arranged activities for the children and teens. Adult adoptees took ownership for, planned, and funded "Call Me Home," an artist showcase, which included films, poetry, multimedia presentations, and dance on the Friday evening prior to the conference. Tom Manvydas helped the artists to obtain sponsorship from *Korean Central Daily Newspaper*. The program was held in the newspaper's auditorium, and the show belonged to the adoptees in every sense. Adoptive parents, Koreans, and Korean Americans were privileged to be invited to share the experience. The Association of Korea Adoptees Los Angeles worked with the Korean American Museum for an adoptee art exhibit held on Sunday afternoon, to which those attending the conference were also invited.

For many, the most memorable session was the panel of birth parents KAAN brought from Korea and one who was currently living in the United States. I realized that only a few years prior, I had not known any adult Korean adoptees. Now I had experienced meeting not only adoptees, but their birth parents as well. For others the fact that the First Lady Lee Hee Ho sent a videotaped message personalized for KAAN and that representatives of the Korean government came all the way from Korea to acknowledge the adoption community and answer their questions was astonishing.

The luncheon was awesome. Our keynote speaker was Washington State Senator Paull Shin who shared his life experience. When Senator Shin was a four-year-old child in Korea, his mother had passed away and his father abandoned him. He struggled as a child on the streets, looking for food and wanting an education. Finally at eighteen, he was adopted by an American Army officer and brought to America where, despite many difficulties, he took advantage of every opportunity that came his way. He finally became both a university professor and the first Korean American state senator. He has continued to inspire those who meet him with his statement, "Blood is thicker than water, but love is thicker than blood."

Also at the luncheon was a video titled *Love and Connection: The story of Jay Trevor*. It was the story of my dear friend Terra Trevor's Korean-born son, Jay who died of cancer. In this video made by the Trevor's Korean American family friend, Korean and American songs alternated throughout the video in much the same way as the Trevors had raised their son. Jay's memorial service had taken place in the Korean American church that

Jay Trevor (center) and his mom, Terra, (to the right of him) were among those meeting Governor Shim Dae Pyung of Chungchongnamdo on our 1998 Family Exchange program trip to Korea.

had offered support and heritage connections to the entire Trevor family for several years. Previous to that, while he was in an earlier remission, I'd had the honor of taking Jay to Korea on the Friends of Korea Family Exchange Program. Jay had seen his motherland before he died.

Perhaps the experience of the first national conference could be summed up in the following statement submitted to us after the conference:

"This conference was unique. I have never experienced anything like it. As an adoptee, who has been isolated from other adoptees and from Koreans, I see a lot of hope. We certainly are more visible. Signed, A conference attendee"

To quote Kathy Beck, adoptive parent from Seattle, "At the first conference we saw that the adoption community we belonged to was much bigger than we had realized, and that there was a place for us in it."

Annual Conferences

For the next few conferences, KAAN continued to develop a template for an inclusive grassroots conference. Our second national conference was held July 21-23, 2000 in Hasbrouck Heights New Jersey. The conference co-chairs were adoptive parent Lindy Gelber and adult adoptee Tom Masters. Once again we had a Korean adoptee artist showcase with Nathalie Mihee Lemoine as curator. Keynote speakers included Phoebe Eng author of *Warrior Lessons* and Miss Pennsylvania, adult adoptee, Susan Spafford. For the first time in the Korean adoption community Deann Borshay presented her film *First Person Plural*. The film shared her life story of searching through multiple identities to find herself. The story brought conference attendees to their feet in a standing ovation.

At the second conference, we continued to struggle with the balance of the needs of adoptees and adoptive parents. Though adoptees had had input into our entire conference program, after reading the reviews of our second conference, it was clear adoptees needed sole ownership of more than the adoptee artist showcase. They also needed a space where any adoptee, and particularly those attending the conference for the first time, felt safe.

At the third conference, held in Seattle July 27–29, 2001, we implemented an adult adoptee only session in each time slot for the first time. Kathy Beck was the adoptive parent in charge, and adopted adult Barbara Kim was responsible for the adult adoptee only programming. In illustration of why adult adoptee only sessions were needed, I will describe a workshop from an earlier conference.

At a previous conference, we had a session titled, "Living and Working in Korea." It consisted of a panel of adult adoptees that were doing just that, living and working in Korea. They wanted to share feelings about their experience and offer resources to other adoptees who also wanted to live and work in Korea. The session was open to everyone, with adoptive parents filling the seats at about a two to one ratio with adoptees. For some of the adoptive parents, the idea of their adopted children someday returning to live and work in Korea was a bit scary. They were quite vocal with their questions about *why* adult adoptees would have returned to live in Korea. The adoptees offering the workshop felt the purpose of their workshop was to reach out to their fellow adoptees in the audience, those who wanted to know *how* to return to live and work in Korea. Adoptees also wanted to hear what that experience felt like. The adoptees felt their space at the conference was being invaded.

We wanted adult adoptees to know we would respect their space. So implementing sessions for adult adoptees only where the focus remained on the needs of adoptees, not adoptive parents, was needed. It took some time for adoptive parents to understand such sessions were not designed to "leave them out." We continued to have workshops where adoptees shared and answered the questions of adoptive parents. It worked well.

Going into our fourth conference which had the theme, "Sharing Strengths to Build Community Partnerships," held July 26-28, 2002 in Minnesota we were excited, because we felt we had the template for carving out the space to meet everyone's individual needs. Because the KAAN conference has a different constituency than other conferences and tries to meet all of those needs, it can be very stressful for those leaders who work on it. In Minnesota, the adoptive parent co-chair for the conference had the additional burden of never having attended a KAAN Conference.

One session that had been requested on the evaluation forms at the Seattle conference was a forum on connecting to the Korean American Community that would include an adoptee, an adoptive parent, and a Korean American. The Korean American and the adoptive parent had been selected for this session. There was a list of suggestions for the adoptee slot, but the adoptive parent leader insisted an adoptee was not necessary for the panel because the adoptive parent she had chosen could speak well for the entire adoption community. KAAN organizers disagreed. Adoptees, who are not children, will speak for themselves. This was the cracking point for the adoptive parent who was co-chairing the conference. She appeared unable to handle the deep feelings of adoptees that were emerging. Her impulse was to try to speak for them. It was over this issue that the adoptive parent resigned.

KAAN leaders thought seriously of canceling the conference, but our adoptee coordinator, Tawni Traynor, never did. She said, "We have not even tried." With that, Tawni rallied her Adopted Korean Connection group. Because Tawni is married to a fellow adult adoptee, we recruited Tawni's mother-in-law to become her adoptive parent conference co-chair, and we pulled the conference together. It was the first year that adult adoptees predominated as attendees. It solidified our direction of KAAN's being a place where adoptees and adoptive parents can have their needs met.

Our fifth conference, "One People, Two Histories: Korean Adoption as Part of One hundred Years of Korean Immigration," took place in Arlington, Virginia, July 25-27, 2003. Hardworking co-chairs were Margie Perscheid, adoptive parent, and Michelle Howard, adult adoptee. Being in our nation's capital made the event extra special, and the conference was well attended by both adoptees and adoptive parents who respected each other's space. We enjoyed a pre-show at the Smithsonian where adoptees, Deborah Johnson, Deann Borshay, and Chris Sonpiet spoke. We finished with a Sunday afternoon reception at the Korean Ambassador's residence.

At the conference in Washington D.C., some parents of adult adoptees attended the conference with their young adult children. In particular, one young adult adoptee and her mother joined me for lunch. It was clear that they were having some intense discussion about family and adoption. I asked them for their suggestions about what kinds of programs KAAN could develop in the future that could facilitate dialogue among adoptive parents and their adult children. The next morning, after the conference had ended, this young adult adoptee and her mother came to me. You could tell by the body language of both of them that they were feeling quite close to each other and both told me the conference had an impact on their relationship. Later the adoptee wrote me a note which said, "I came to the KAAN conference to be part of the adoption community and to connect with other adoptees. I never expected to end up feeling closer to my mother."

This interaction affected our design of the sixth conference, "Building Connections, Honoring Differences," held July 23-25, 2004, in San Francisco. For the first time we had a couple of sessions for parents of adult adoptees only—"Redefining Ourselves: How to Parent from an Emptying Nest" and "Giving Our Children Custody of Their Own Lives: Parenting Young Adopted Adults." These sessions offered support to me personally, because my adopted children had become young adults. I had the chance to discuss with my peers how it feels for me at this life stage. It was nice to be in a session not geared to the needs of the parents of younger children. We each need programs that are just for us. We also started an exciting new program for young adult adoptees ages eighteen to twenty-two. While I was with my friends, my daughter participated in the young adult adoptee dinner and a couple of programs focused for their age group. Young adult adoptee Camille Beck decided on the content of the program.

In San Francisco, it was my turn to co-chair the conference again. I was delighted to work with Carolyn Scholl, an adopted adult who is also vice president of the Association of Korean Adoptees Southern

Workshop at the 2004 KAAN Conference in San Francisco.

California, as my co-chair. It was wonderful to be in San Francisco with its Asian neighborhoods.

The seventh conference, "Seoul Searching—The Life of Adoption," held July 22–24, 2005 in the Detroit area, went beyond our expectations. It met all the philosophical goals we have for the conference, which include strengthening connections within the local community and extending the national network. It was an interesting and thought-provoking conference with something for everyone, strengthening relationships among the diverse set of groups we serve. The local Michigan team understood the goals, were focused, and worked well together. Those working on the conference included: Jen Hilzinger, adoptive parent, Kate Hers, adult adoptee, Rachel Jones, young adult adoptee, and Dr. Sook Wilkinson, Korean American. For the first several years, we worked on the template for a balance between adoptee and adoptive parent needs. In Detroit, our interactions with the Korean American Community became more reciprocal and more worthwhile due to the efforts of Korean American psychologist, Dr. Sook Wilkinson. Tack-Yong Kim of Michigan Weekly arranged a golf outing that raised substantial funds for our conference. Dominic Pangborn held a fundraiser at his art gallery. Joseph Hwang from Korean American Culture Center allowed us to use their center for our youth program.

However, we also faced a bigger predicament. We had been unable to find a hotel near enough to the airport to provide shuttle service. The fee for transportation in one direction was fifty dollars per person. In order for our conference to be economically feasible, we needed a shuttle service. Reverend Christian Oh, president of the Michigan Council of Korean Churches, arranged for church vans to transport our speakers and conference attendees from the airport. All day on the Friday preceding the conference they went back and forth, dealing with flight delays, language barriers, and multiple airport terminals, working to bring our adoption community together. It was an effort of the heart. With a concern for reciprocity, KAAN was able to make some small financial donations to the Michigan Council of Korean Churches and the Korean American Culture Center. I am sure that those donations they had not requested and didn't expect were welcome to them. However, in making Korean American connections, they work best when the Korean American organizations determine for themselves what is meaningful to them.

What Reverend Christian Oh wanted to do was to offer a prayer for us at our Saturday night dinner. Whether one is Christian or not, one can appreciate Reverend Oh's effort to show his love and concern for the adoption community. Seventy-five percent of Korean Americans are practicing Christians. They were expressing their outreach to the adoption community in the way that made sense from their perspective on adoption. My hope is that those Korean American church members who helped us with transportation felt

Korean American supporters of the 2005 KAAN Conference included: (left to right) Dominic Pangborn, Joseph Hwang, Dr. Sook Wilkinson, Reverend Christian Oh, Tack-Yong Kim, and State Representative Hoon-Yung Hopgood.

appreciated. I hope they felt a closer connection to adoptees who share their blood, to whom they feel some emotional connection, but who they usually cannot reach.

More KAAN conferences are already in the planning stage. From June 30 to July 2, 2006, our conference, "Han Ma Eum: One Heart and One Mind," will be held in Seoul, Korea. Because of its location we will have unique access to resources for this conference, offering conference attendees opportunities to learn more about birth families, adoption from a Korean perspective and to really learn about Korea itself. Our hope is domestic Korean adoptive families will join with us in the conference. On

July 20-22, 2007, the KAAN Conference will be held in Boston. We are hoping for a tenth anniversary conference in 2008 in Los Angeles. Who knows what else the future holds for KAAN? Whatever it is, it will reflect the voices of the adoption community, working toward our primary goal of deepening understanding between, and enhancing relationships among, adoption community members.

What KAAN Has Become

KAAN has continued to be a project of Friends of Korea, which acts as the nonprofit organization housing KAAN and supporting the conference. Somewhat like the Olympics, the conference itself belongs each year to the local community in the city in which it is held. The conference allows those groups in a local area to share their community with others nationally. Individuals and representatives of groups from other locations have the opportunity to meet and share with others from all over the United States, other countries, and Korea. They can talk with others about the structure of their local groups and get ideas for new programs, as well as attending workshops on heritage and adoption issues. Each group no longer has to reinvent everything themselves, but they can learn about what someone somewhere else has already done.

Those in the Korean adoption community strongly resist others speaking for them. KAAN is not the sole builder of a network under its control. Because only adoptees fully understand the adoptee's experience, only adoptive parents fully understand the adoptive parent experience, and only Korean and Korean Americans fully understand their experiences, we cannot speak for each other. KAAN is not, never has been, and could not be *the* voice of adopted adult Koreans. KAAN is not a support group for adoptive families acting as *the* voice of adoptive families. KAAN provides a space where others can speak for themselves, so that those within the adoption community can relate to and understand each other better. In the interest of bringing our diverse community together, KAAN does not take stands on issues, but allows all views to be represented at our conference and in our weekly email newsletter.

The value of KAAN lies in giving individuals who are willing to work with others the opportunity to continue to strengthen and extend the network that has a life of its own. The KAAN conference gives visibility and voice to the individuals who make up the Korean adoption community at a national and international level. KAAN has shown itself to be viable and consistent. KAAN acts as a bridge on which adoptees, adoptive families, Koreans and Korean Americans can stand to interact with and better understand each other.

Each year, those for whom the KAAN conference has meaning work on it nationally. Those in the community where the conference is held have significant ownership of the program content and fundraising responsibilities. Funding has continued to be, and I believe will always be, a struggle. Because of the grassroots nature and community ownership of the conference, registration fees have been kept low, so that it is less of a financial hardship for people to attend. We have let the registration fees creep up some to take some of the burden of fundraising off, but the fee is still significantly below the actual cost per person of the conference. KAAN considers its membership to be anyone connected to Korean adoption. There is no membership fee.

What Individuals Get out of KAAN

For me, the Korean American Adoptee Adoptive Family Network has allowed me to reach outside of isolation and connect with others across the country to fully be a member of an adoption community. There were many things that I as a Euro-American adoptive parent could not personally give to my children because of our ethnic difference and because of the difference in the way we experience adoption. What adoptive parents can give to their children are resources. Through KAAN I have had the chance to work with others to offer resources, not only to my own children, but to their peers. It makes everything worth it when I read comments such as this one from young adopted adult Kathleen Dunham:

"Being part of KAAN for the last few years has been an experience that has helped me be the person I am today. It is a time when I am so proud to be who I am. I am able to discuss issues only other Korean adoptees would understand. KAAN is really something special. It makes me feel alive and proud to be Korean. I don't have that feeling anywhere else. I think KAAN is such an important thing for all Korean adoptees, young and old. It has such a diverse group of adoptees; some from the West Coast, some from the East Coast, and everything in between. I get to talk with Koreans from all over and make some really great connections that, hopefully, I will keep for life. One of the best things about KAAN is it is not just a 'culture camp,' not to say they are bad, but at a certain point it is great to move on in the Korean identity process and develop a deeper meaning of what it is to be a Korean adoptee. I have had some really great times at KAAN and hope more Korean adoptees my age will come and participate. I live in an area where there are very, very few minorities, and KAAN is a really great outlet for me to be who I am, express who I am, be proud of who I am, and never feel guilty, or ashamed of who I am. I feel understood and accepted. I would suggest KAAN to anyone who is willing to open themselves to learn, to teach, to grow."

Kathleen Dunham (center) with fellow adoptees Sloane Tabisel (left) and Sara Campbell (right).

These words of Kathleen Dunham fill my heart with joy. At the beginning of our adoption experience, I was told our family would be forever changed. Over time I am learning what that really means. The KAAN conference is unique in that it has grown with my family as we have grown. KAAN still offers support for groups with their focus on how to adopt and the coming together of young families. KAAN also supports those of us who have grown past this stage. I have been able to form friendships with parents of adult adoptees who have walked this path with me. We have watched our children struggle at various times with the challenges of our mutual experience. We are able to be honest with each other and share our joys and fears. We learn from each other. I am grateful for special friends from all over the world I never would have met without the network. Even a kitchen knife cannot carve its own handle, we need others who share our life experience.

Connected to Two Countries

고래 싸움에 새우 등 터진다

A shrimp will be crushed when two whales fight.
KOREAN PROVERB

Moses and Intercountry Adoption

A long time ago in Egypt, Pharaoh's daughter went down to the river to wash and found a Hebrew baby floating among the bulrushes in the Nile. When the baby cried, Pharaoh's daughter had compassion on him, named him, loved him, and raised him as her own child. Yet, somewhere deep inside himself, perhaps because of questions about his birth family, his experience with racism, and the frictions between two peoples, the Hebrews and the Egyptians, Moses could never forget he was a Hebrew. When he was grown Moses saw an Egyptian beating a Hebrew. Moses slew the Egyptian and hid him under the sand, thinking no one had seen him. However, Moses had been seen. Ultimately, Pharaoh called for Moses to be killed. It was then that the God of the Hebrews delivered a series of plagues upon the Egyptians, until Pharaoh was forced to let Moses and his people go.

I retell this story from the Bible, because many people are familiar with it, and for me it has been instructive about what adoption could possibly feel like to some adoptees. Perhaps the reader can avoid initial judgments about whether or not the story parallels his own story or parallels the adoption interchange between the countries in his own situation. Remember this is a book about perspective. Here is an opportunity to "jump out of the water," "climb out of the well," or choose any other metaphor you like for seeing the world from a different perspective. The story of Moses is a familiar story from the perspective of an interethnic adoptee. It illustrates how an adoptee could possibly come to view his adoption. In this story the adoption not only saves Moses' life, but also affirms the life he lived was worthwhile. I wonder if his adoptive family saw it that way. Pharaoh's daughter's perspective as she suffered from various plagues that befell her was likely different. She lost a son she had raised, perhaps through no individual fault of her own.

The story of Moses shows the complexity of an adoption across ethnic lines. In my experience, intercountry adoption has not allowed me to avoid far-away birth parents and adoption issues; instead it has added additional layers of challenge to the lives of everyone in my family. I don't repeat the story as a warning to adoptive families not to adopt, though some may see it that way. I don't repeat the story to terrify those who have already adopted and have young children. I repeat the story because it has helped me to process and understand the issues I have encountered in my family's experience with intercountry adoption. My hope is that this story can help others understand the issues of being connected to two countries as well.

For me, the story of Moses reveals the inherent issues in an adoption between two peoples, between two countries. In addition to the challenges in parenting any child, there are three additional layers. First, there is the adoption issue. Why was this child available for adoption? What happened to the birth family? What kind of choice was made by the birthmother?

Second, in an interracial adoption the child is visibly different from the adoptive family and experiences racism not faced by the adoptive parents. This brings in another layer of identity issues. Third, the child is connected to two countries, and the relationships between those two countries matter to adoptees and to adoptive families.

Support for Birth Families

Let's examine the Moses story more closely. Why was Moses in the bulrushes to begin with? At the beginning of the story, Pharaoh had given the order that all male Hebrew children be killed at birth. He did this because the population of Hebrews within Egypt was beginning to approach the numbers of the Egyptians themselves, raising a security concern. In other words, when Moses' birthmother chose to place him for adoption, it really was not a choice. She had to relinquish him to save his life.

The first issue raised in the Moses model is whether or not birth families have a choice in placing children. When birth families do not have social support for raising their children, children can be separated from birth families unnecessarily. The separation can be dramatic, as in China, where the government's one child policy and cultural norms result in the abandonment of baby girls. It can be coercive, as it has sometimes been in Korea, where birth parents have been pressured to relinquish children for a "better life." It can be enticing because there is economic advantage to the government of the sending country in allowing their country to escape the economic strain of building a social welfare system. Adoptive parents have the economic advantage over birth parents.

Koreans now living in a thriving country are examining these issues. In December 2002, I had the chance to be part of a conference in Seoul sponsored by CARITAS. Their website states CARITAS is a confederation of 162 Catholic relief, development, and social service organizations working to build a better world, especially for the poor and oppressed, in over 200 countries and territories. The theme of the conference was "Taking Care of Our Children Ourselves." In Sun Park from Ehwa Women's University gave the keynote speech. She kindly handed me an English translation. She spoke allegorically of a village on a river. Every so often she explained a child would be found floating down the river almost drowned. People from the village would swim out to save the child. They saved most of them, but sadly not all. Over time more and more children were found in the river, too many for the village to rescue them all. Perhaps, the villagers decided, it was time to go up river and see where the children were coming from in the first place. So the theme of the conference was how to confront why Korean children were available for adoption and to explore social supports that would make adoption unnecessary.

Support for Domestic Adoption in Korea

If the birth parents are unavailable, do Koreans have the opportunity to raise Korean-born children in need of adoption? Following the conference, I visited a CARITAS facility and had the chance to meet a Korean adoptive parent and her toddler son. The facility had recently been remodeled. During remodeling, they had placed the babies temporarily in the homes of foster families. The family who cared for this little boy could not bring themselves to return him when the facility was finished, and so they adopted him. They had two older daughters and this little boy. It reminded me of the foster care to adoption system in the United States and caused me to wonder why it was not more common in Korea. In talking with this little

A domestic adoptive mom and her little boy at the CARITAS facility in December 2002.

boy's mother, she told me how she had carefully chosen a name for her son. It reminded me of the naming stories of American adoptive parents including myself. Some things we share.

In August 2004, I once again visited Korea, taking travelers on the Friends of Korea Family Exchange Program. On this trip most of our logistical and support needs were met by International Korean Adoptee Services (InKAS). When I arrived in Korea I found that Aie Ree Jung of InKAS, believing post placement support is important for all adoptive families even if they share an ethnicity, got a grant from the city of Seoul for a weekend camp for domestic Korean adoptive families. I was privileged to attend the first evening of the camp and to interact with the Korean families as a fellow adoptive parent. In many ways, watching those Korean families in their matching T-shirts, I saw myself back in my own early years as an adoptive parent with young children at our Hand In Hand support group. The challenge of being seen as real families, of helping others to know what we know in our hearts, that these are our children, remains the same for all adoptive families anywhere in the world. Yet, these adoptive families sharing an ethnicity, were not facing the extra levels of difference interethnic, intercountry adoptive families face.

In all of these instances concerning domestic adoption in Korea, I felt privileged to be included, but in many respects, it was not my business. Koreans are responsible for taking care of Korean children. I am an interested outsider. While feeling that the domestic adoption that is occurring in Korea ought to be encouraged, I don't feel that I can make judgments about what is best for Korean children. As an American adoptive parent I am not a neutral, disinterested party. Adoptees will make judgments about whether or not they should have been placed for adoption outside of their birth country. My children's judgments about why they were placed for adoption affect their sense of who they are, and ultimately their relationship with me. This is why it matters to me that Korean children are placed for adoption for the right reasons. The economic disparity between Korean birth parents and American adoptive parents also matters when adoptees examine whether or not their Korean parents had a choice in placing them. No matter how carefully adoptive parents choose the words to explain their children's adoption to them, as adults they will make their own decisions about whether or not their birth parents had a choice. Whether adoptees feel their birth parents had a choice in placing them for adoption doesn't depend on how much adoptive parents love their adopted children, how well they have raised them, or how carefully they told their stories. It will depend on a mix of factors inside and outside of parental control. I accept my children's right as adults to process this information for themselves, even if they come to conclusions different than my own. I will grant them the time it takes to do this processing, a privilege that belongs to them anyway and is not mine to grant.

Which Line Do We Stand In?

The second issue the Moses story brings up is the role racism plays in creating issues for adoptive families. Korean Adoptees face racism while growing up in America. In 1988 upon our return from Korea with our then new daughter Diana, we exited the plane, tired from our journey. As we came to the point where our passports needed to be stamped indicating our reentry to the United States, there were two lines from which to choose. One line was for U.S. citizens and legal residents, the other for new immigrants. Of course, my husband, my son Alexis, and myself were citizens, but our daughter wasn't. We looked at the two lines. The one for citizens was longer, but the one for new immigrants was not moving at all. Exhausted we were hoping to get home as soon as possible.

"She's with us," my husband said, as we moved toward the line for U.S citizens.

We were quickly redirected to the new immigrants line, where we waited and waited. Finally an agent was free and came to process those in our line. The processing took longer because it involved some steps for getting our daughter's "green card" which would be mailed to us. When the card came, it was not green, and it included Diana's picture. The instructions said she should keep the card with her at all times. The card gave her the right to work in the United States. We joked about pinning the card to her diaper and sending her out to supplement the family income.

In 1988, children adopted from other countries did not automatically become U.S. citizens because of the adoption. In order for Diana to stand in the line for U.S citizens, we had to complete the paperwork process after her adoption was final. After completing the paperwork, we were called for an interview at the Immigration and Naturalization Service, where she was pronounced a citizen. I made her a red and white dress with a broad white collar bordered with blue stars. We took her picture eating apple pie and ice cream. We repeated the process a couple of years later for David, except he wanted a cake with a flag on it. We were lucky, unlike a few of our friends who waited years to get their paperwork through for citizenship; our children had quickly become legal Americans.

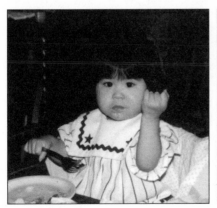

Diana becomes a U.S. citizen on February 10, 1989. Alexis welcomes David as a new U.S. citizen on March 5, 1991.

Adoptees and Americanness

For some intercountry adoptees the citizenship process was never completed. For whatever reason, their families never realized they had family members who were standing in a different line. The most egregious case is that of Joao Herbert. Adopted as an eight-year-old in 1987 from Brazil, Joao learned English, forgot Portuguese, and became Americanized. Though he was legally adopted, he never became a U.S. citizen. Two months after his high school graduation, he was arrested for selling seven-and-a-half ounces of marijuana and was subsequently deported to Brazil. Unequipped to function in Brazil, with no meaningful connections or support system, Joao Herbert was found four years later shot to death in slums sixty miles from Sao Paolo, Brazil. Korean adoptee, Aaron Billings hopefully will not face the same fate. Adopted at the age of three, Aaron completed high school in special education classes. Aaron has not always exercised good judgment in making friends. He was arrested for accepting a ride in a stolen car and for selling one marijuana cigarette. His deportation has been ordered, but Aaron has disappeared. These are two examples of adoptees whose Americanness was not even legally guaranteed.

The Child Citizenship Act, which went into effect on February 27, 2001, granted citizenship for international adoptees who were under the age of eighteen. Despite the efforts of some, such as adoptive parent Jan King in Alabama and adult adoptee Carolyn Scholl in San Diego, the new law did not include adoptees over the age of eighteen whose parents had failed to obtain citizenship for them. Racism against Asians in this country has often included the component of Asians not being seen as fully American. In some cases we have adoptees convicted of minor crimes who have been "sent back where they came from." Adoptees did not emigrate of their own free will. While it is nice adoptees coming from other countries in the future will have their rights protected by an act of Congress, there are those already here from earlier years whose future has not been ensured. Despite the act of Congress, the underlying racism has not changed.

Adoptees as Korean Americans

Adoptees are not alone in becoming immigrants from Korea, of course. The first Korean to become an American citizen was Philip Jaisohn, who came to the United States in 1885. He was the first Korean American to become a doctor, receiving his degree in 1892. Though he became a Korean American, his heart remained in Korean causes. He returned to Korea to establish a newspaper and to support Korean independence. He only returned to the United States when he was exiled from Korea. He experienced the tug of belonging to two countries.

It took many years, though, before the first wave of meaningful Korean immigration history occurred in 1903. Korean men were recruited to work on Hawaii's sugar plantations, as they were thought to be harder workers than the Chinese and Japanese who preceded them. These Korean plantation workers were joined by "picture brides" from Korea. These were women who came to Hawaii to marry the Korean men after a process of exchanging pictures.

Because of acts of Congress restricting immigration from Asia, the second wave of Korean immigration didn't occur until the Korean War. In 1952, the McCarran-Walter Act allowed Asians to immigrate in small numbers and eventually to become U.S. citizens. This enabled the second wave of Korean immigration in the 1950s which included Korean-born wives of U.S. servicemen, children sent for adoption, and professional workers and students.

The third wave of Korean immigration began after the signing of The Immigration Act Of 1965. Passed by Congress and signed by Lyndon Johnson, this act did away with the previous harsh restrictions against immigration from Asian countries. The third wave allowed for families of previous immigrants to join them, as well as for professionals to immigrate for employment. This third wave of Korean immigration formed the large Korean American communities in Los Angeles, New York, and Chicago, as well as many smaller ones.

We may note two things. First, a major discrimination that occurred against Asians was they were not allowed to enter the United States and become citizens in the same way as immigrants from Europe. The continuing vestige of that is that Asians who become citizens are seen as less American. This perception extends to Asian-born children, sometimes making it difficult for them to be "just Americans."

Secondly, Korean adoptees were missing from studies and histories of Korean Americans until only recently. As I mentioned previously, in 1996 I attended a conference on Korean American youth and their ethnic identity that made no mention of adoptees as a segment of that youth. There was no acknowledgement adoptees didn't disappear after leaving Korea, but that they still exist as part of the Korean American community. Often for the Korean adoptees, a meaningful sense of connectedness to the Korean American community is missing. This might not matter so much, except for the fact that adoptees are visibly Korean American.

From the story of Moses, I see it is important to care about how Korean Americans are treated within this country because my children are a part of that community, whether they like it or not, whatever their comfort level. When racism occurs against Korean Americans, it affects my family. It also matters to me that Korean American communities reach out to include the adoption community as a part of the greater Korean American community. When this doesn't happen, adoptees can be caught between the two communities, feeling as though they do not really belong to either.

Adoptees are individuals and they resolve their life experiences each in their own fashion. Some, because of their own resilience and outlook, are prominent as Americans. Adoptees such as Hoon-yung Hopgood, Paula

Trout, Mimi McAndrews, and Paull Shin have become state congressmen, congresswomen or senators. United States Marine Corps Lance Corporal Brad Shuder felt American in every sense of the word. Adopted at age twenty-two months from Korea, Brad became the first Korean American to give his life in Iraq on April 12, 2004. Being in the Marine Corps was his dream. Because he lived in my own small community of El Dorado Hills, California, I observed the outreach from the El Dorado Hills community to his family following his death. We have two rocks in our community that are often painted to mark holidays or community events. Following Brad's death, our rocks were painted in his honor and people began to leave flowers, flags, and other mementos there in his memory. The fire station marquee memorialized him. He indeed belonged to his community and to his country by adoption.

"The Rocks" in El Dorado Hills newly painted in memory of Brad Shuder in April 2004, before a flood of flowers surrounded them.

While it is wonderful some adoptees are able to feel completely connected as Americans, I have accepted that some do not feel this way. Because it was not the choice of adoptees to emigrate in the first place, because they have faced racism within this country, because some of them were not even given citizenship, I understand why adoptees might have a range of feelings about their "fit" in America. While my children were growing up, I wanted to be open enough so they would feel free to share the racism they experienced with me. So that I could understand their feelings better, I have tried to learn about myself as a member of the ethnic majority in this country. I try to be willing to listen and learn and not make judgments solely from my own perspective.

Adoptees in Korea

The third issue raised by the story of Moses is the fact adoptees are connected to two countries. I asked David, Diana, and also Alexis, the following question, "Of all the 'Korean things' we did as you were growing up, what was the most important?" All three of them gave me the same answer. The trips to Korea were the most important to them. I have heard the same response from several other adopted adults I know. Despite the age of their arrival, adoptees remain connected to two countries.

Because of the Friends of Korea Family Exchange Program, my children each have had the opportunity to visit Korea several times. The program matches an American adoptive family with a Korean family in the hopes a friendship may grow between them. The American family stays in the home of the Korean family for a few days at the beginning of their trip to Korea before going on the tour portion. Later, the Korean family may visit the American family in America. Each of my three children got to travel to Korea a few times at various ages from eight to late teens. At each age they seemed to derive something different. When they were eight, I didn't worry that they

Diana explores Chonan with her favorite author, Marie Lee.

couldn't deeply appreciate the museums or cultural artifacts. They were getting to know Koreans. What they gained was a sense that Korea was not so foreign—that it was a fun place to visit where they could find a comfort level, as Americans.

In sorting out the mix of their identities, some adoptees return on their own to live in Korea as adults. Adoptees who return to Korea will find a support system, unlike that available to adoptees from any other country. Likely if Aaron Billings were deported, he would find resources which were unavailable to Joao Herbert in Brazil.

In April 2005, I visited Korea in an effort to better understand the support programs and organizations that exist for adoptees in Korea. These support systems exist because adoptees returning to Korea worked for them and because the Korean government was responsive. I am glad adoptees living in Korea have laid groundwork for those who will come after them. Adoptees in Korea can meet and support each other through an adoptee-run organization in Korea called G.O.A.'L. This organization was developed by adoptees themselves to help adoptees adjust to living and working in Korea, sharing a sense of adoptee community in their motherland. On their webpage they state, "More importantly, G.O.A.'L's presence in Korea fosters awareness about adoption in the Korean government, adoption agencies, and Korean society."

Adoptee Solidarity Korea (ASK) is another group formed by adoptees in Korea. ASK is an adoptee membership-based organization that holds weekly meetings, seeking to foster leadership in each of its members. The goals of ASK are: to create greater public awareness of issues related to adoption by providing resources and educational opportunities; to empower adoptees to develop their own critical analysis; to increase the profile of the adoptee community to one that has a political voice. The mission of Adoptee Solidarity Korea (ASK) is to raise awareness to the systematic problems of intercountry adoption out of Korea and the socio-political solutions that will be necessary to bring it to an end.

Another meaningful service organization for adoptees that has arisen is InKAS. InKAS acts as a bridge for Korean Adoptees and adoptive families

Chris with Aie ree Jung, president of InKAS December 2002 in Seoul.

returning to Korea. With their small budget, but tremendous heart, they have done a lot. InKAS founder, Aie Ree Jung, grew up playing with the children at the orphanage in Mokpo. Mr. Yune Chi-ho, Ms. Jung's grandfather, established Gongsaengwon, and her parents continued to run the orphanage to this day. As a child, Ms. Jung couldn't stop thinking about the children from Gongsaengwon who had to leave their birth country. When Ms. Jung, who majored in social welfare in college, saw adoptees visiting Korea, she wanted to offer good resources and services to them. All the services InKAS provides are free of charge. Recently InKAS negotiated health care support for adoptees living in Korea.

KoRoot is a guesthouse for adoptees who may want to stay up to a month. This is a great place for those adoptees who return to Korea for an extended period of time, to stay while they are making the transition to living in Korea. For only fifteen dollars a night, the guesthouse provides all the services you would expect from a youth hostel, but with a focus on adoptees needs. On their website you can see the beauty of this house located near Kyung-Bok Palace, which is run by Reverend Do Hyun Kim.

The Global Adoption Information & Post Service Center provides connections to all four of

KoRoot guesthouse in Seoul.

the Korean Adoption Agencies for birth family search support and other post adoption services. Several of the universities offer Korean programs for foreigners, while Inje University offers a special program for adoptees. The YMCA and the Overseas Koreans foundation also have summer programs for adoptees

For our family the best connections have been personal connections to individual Koreans and their families. I am glad we have personal connections in Korea should my son decide to explore living there, because moving to another country is not easy. Even with the adoptee support and the organizations that have arisen, the language and cultural differences will be great. If adoptees choose to live in Korea, there can be some struggle for them to feel as though they are accepted and belong.

When we were completing the interviews with the social worker for our first adoption, she asked a question, "How would you feel if your child grew up and decided to return to live in Korea?"

Our answer was, "How could that happen? We will raise her as an American."

We had no capacity to visualize the possibility, and there wasn't further discussion on this topic. If asked today, I would explore this question in more depth.

Complexity for Adoptive Families

While it has been important to me to try to understand and empathize with the experience my children are having as adoptees, as an adoptive parent I have also been having an adoption experience. I have my own feelings to process. I first had Korea enter my life when our family traveled to Korea to bring home our first Korean-born child. I had never traveled outside the United States and was terrified. Yet, I cherished the right for my husband and me to bring our child home ourselves, rather than having her escorted through our adoption agency, which was what adoptive families were expected to do at the time. Somehow my husband and I knew in a deep and emotional way that we needed to touch Korea.

As Korea had offered us this opportunity to expand our family, we realized that in the future visiting and learning about Korea would not be like visiting or learning about any other country. We knew the connection for our family was going to run much deeper. As the years progressed we found this emotional connection to Korea never diminished. We bought our kids cultural artifacts from Korea. We bought a Young Chang piano—just because it was Korean. We began to have our ears perk up when Korea was in the news. We reached out to make Korean friends. We saw Korea almost as fairyland, our connection to which ended the challenges of infertility, giving us the chance to be a family. In this magical place, my husband and I became parents twice again, and our birth child gained a sister and a brother.

Both times we went to Korea to bring our children home to America we fell in love. First we fell in love with our children, who we felt were destined to be ours. But, the falling in love also went beyond our children; it extended to Korea itself. We were so well treated in Korea. On the way home with our daughter, the agent checking us in on Korean Airlines put a special "first class" tag on our luggage. Though we didn't have first class tickets, she said, "You are first class people." It felt as though the whole country was cheering for us.

Because adopting from Korea was such a wonderful experience for us, we wanted to share the experience with everyone. I fell in love without realizing how American centered my view of the world was and often still is. Korea is not fairyland. It is a sovereign nation—not an extension of the United States. By adopting children from Korea, my husband and I brought the complexity of emotionally resolving dual national connections into their lives and into our own.

Experiencing Anti-Americanism

In September 2002, the New York Times had the following headline: "Korean Mob Briefly Detains U.S. Soldier After Subway Fight." I read an American soldier, Private Murhpy, refused to accept a leaflet being distributed on a Seoul subway. The article said he refused the leaflet because it was in Korean. He doesn't read Korean. The leaflets were being distributed in response to an incident that occurred on June 13, 2002.

On that date a U.S. minesweeping vehicle ran over Shin Hyo-soon and Shim Mi-seon. The two girls were on their way to a friend's birthday party in the northern city of Uijeongbu. They were only fourteen years old. General Leon LaPorte, commander of U.S. forces in South Korea, immediately apologized after the accident. The driver and the track commander of the minesweeping vehicle were charged with negligent homicide. On August 1, Secretary of State Colin Powell again apologized for the incident. However, some South Koreans remained dissatisfied, demanding the 37,000 U.S. troops stationed in South Korea leave the country. From his refusal to accept the leaflet the situation escalated. In the end, demonstrators abducted Private Murphy for several hours. He was taken to a rally and forced to make public statements in accordance with demonstrators' demands.

On my visit to South Korea in August 2002, I found myself inadvertently in a rally connected to the accident that killed the two young Korean girls. A mockup tank appeared, in which a student wearing a papier-mâché U.S. soldier's head and holding an upside

The beginning of an anti-American demonstration in Seoul in August 2002.

down American flag was riding. Being curious, and wanting to think about it more later, I took a picture of the tank before student protestors came through with megaphones. Before I knew it I was the only blonde-haired person in a throng. Though there had been many demonstrations regarding the deaths of the two Korean girls, suddenly being on the spot, so to speak, was frightening and surreal, primarily because I was very aware of my own physical appearance.

I cannot imagine what it might have been like had I been taken, as that U.S. soldier had been, into the crowd and asked to account for American foreign policy. Suddenly I was pondering, what responsibilities do individuals have for the actions of their government? What responsibilities do individuals have for others of their ethnicity? How do others of my ethnicity represent or misrepresent me? If I were to be taken as a token American, how would I react? From my American perspective, the accident that killed the two young Korean girls was clearly that, an accident. I feel loyalty to my own native land. I cannot escape the skin I am in. Yet, I was standing among people with a different life experience, a different perspective. More than that, I felt connection to these people because of my children.

Chris with fellow guests of the Korean government in November 2002.

I returned to Korea again in late November 2002. I was the guest of the Korean government on a trip sponsored by the Overseas Koreans Foundation for four Americans who had contributed to promoting the value of Korean heritage in the Unites States. My fellow travelers were: Vernon Gray, speaker of the Howard County Assembly near Washington D.C.; Franklin P. Hall, assemblyman of the state of Virginia; Kevin J. O'Toole, assemblyman of the state of New Jersey; and some of their family members. Assemblyman O'Toole brought his wife Beth and his parents. Kevin O'Toole's parents had met in Korea when his father was serving in the U.S. military. Assemblyman Franklin Hall's wife Phoebe also accompanied us. It was a study in contrasts to be visiting Korea during a time when anti-Americanism was most evident, and yet be there because the Korean government wanted to reach out to Americans. The volatility and value of free speech is not only an American phenomenon.

The two U.S. soldiers responsible for the minesweeping vehicle that ran over the two girls had just been acquitted by the U.S. military court. Demonstrators marched on U.S. bases and threw firebombs at them. There were signs in some restaurants saying "Americans not welcome." I took a train down to Cholla province with Korean friends. On the train, a man yelled and cursed at one of the young women traveling with me for speaking English to me.

Mikuk Bandae (We are against America). Chris reads this spray painted sign on the ground at the train station in Kwangju, Cholla Province on an earlier trip to Korea in summer 2000.

The Korean presidential election was in full force. As I read the English editions of the *Korea Times* and the *Korea Herald*, Mr. Noh, the ultimate victor in the election, appeared to be appealing to anti-American sentiments. I had a chance to talk with Korean students about their feelings. Some told me they felt closer to North Korea than to America because they were of the same blood. Others told me they were angry because they felt America did not respect Korea. In fact, I saw this was the prevailing view of most after we had talked for awhile. They felt the tanks that killed the two girls did so by accident. They said they felt American forces were in Korea for the good of Korea, as well as for American interest. But, they said, despite apologies, America was not sorry two fourteen-year-old girls had been killed. I could see the potential for difficulties between our two countries.

Processing My Experiences with Anti-Americanism

The incidents I have related occurred against the background of other historical incidents reflecting the rough spots that have periodically arisen in the relationship between South Korea and the United States since the division of Korea following World War II. To learn more about these incidents, I would suggest reading books such as *The Two Koreas* by Don Oberdorfer, *The Kwangju Uprising* by Henry Scott-Stokes and Lee Jae Eui, and *Massive Entanglement, Marginal Influence* by William Gleysteen Jr. I came to terms with the anti-Americanism I experienced in Korea by acknowledging that, while having a special connection to Korea, I am an American, and more than that, an American whose Americanness is not questioned.

It was unusual for me to experience anti-Americanism in Korea. If I had stayed on the tour bus, I would not have experienced it. Even off the tour bus, I have never been treated as well as I have been in Korea by friends and their friends alike. Still, for me, the potential for emotional challenge is there. If adoptive families have not traveled to Korea or explored the depth of their connection, do they find the emotional concern of potential conflict between our countries to be less? I believe it may be the case. But, to several adoptees I have talked with it matters if Korea and the United States get along. Particularly adoptees with thoughts of birth families have seemed concerned. Speaking at the Smithsonian in a pre-show to the 2003 KAAN conference in Washington D.C., adult adoptee Deann Borshay made an impassioned plea for a peaceful solution to the nuclear problem in North Korea. Having reunited with her birth family, and being still in the process of getting to know them, how scary it must have been for her to face the thought of losing them again.

"Will We Get Along?"

Symbolic of their life experience, adoptees stand in the line for foreigners when they return to Korea. As an adoptive parent I stand with my children in the line for foreigners when we visit Korea, but our feelings about this may not be the same. I have always been a foreigner in Korea. There was a time when my children were not. With my children, I share the hope the divide between Korea and the United States will not become too great. I hope to avoid the differences between two peoples that occurred in the story of Moses.

At the first KAAN conference, held July 1999 in Los Angeles, California, our keynote speaker was Washington State Senator Paull Shin. He spoke inspirationally as one of the first Korean Adoptees sharing his life story. Near the end of his speech he was talking about his political career and shared he had been a candidate to be a U.S. ambassador to South Korea. He was one of twenty-seven candidates who had made it to be one of three finalists. During the interview he was asked which side he would take if there were to be a conflict between South Korea and the United States.

Senator Shin answered by saying America was to him his fatherland with the many opportunities it has given to him. Korea was his motherland. Senator Shin said, "As a son, which side would you take? What I as

Chris attending the Korean Consulate's reception for new president Noh Moo Hyun at the Asian Art Museum in San Francisco in spring 2003. Like Senator Shin, Chris hopes for a continued good relationship between the United States and South Korea.

a son want is for my mom and dad to get along most beautifully."

Like Senator Shin, it has been my deep wish that Korea and America will always get along most beautifully. The reality is parents sometimes don't get along with each other, to the point of divorcing. When there is discord between Korea and the United States, there are ramifications for adoptees and adoptive families. Because I adopted my children from another country, circumstances may develop that will make that connection uncomfortable for myself or for my child. That is just the way it is.

A Cooperative Model of Intercountry Adoption

An alternative to what occurred in the story of Moses is a relationship of mutually beneficial cooperation between birth families and adoptive families, between ethnicities, and between countries. One hundred thousand Korean children have been adopted into the United States. With their extended families, they form a Korean American adoption community of over two million. This could be a powerful force in support of Korean Americans when racism occurs. These folks could have an interest in buying Korean products, in trips to Korea, and in improving cross-cultural understanding.

I believe that to achieve this model of cooperation, everyone has to have a greater awareness of the issues involved. This awareness cannot be only on the surface. To achieve that level of understanding takes work not just among adoptive parents, but also among Koreans and Korean Americans. The idea is that Korea could bring adoptive families together rather than pulling them apart—that adoptees could have connection to all their heritages. In this model, children would only be placed for adoption when their birth family truly could not care for them. Children would be placed into adoptive families who understood the needs of their children and had the capability to take steps to meet those needs. Preparation would be there before the adoption. Post-placement support would be there following the adoption.

From my experience in knowing adoptive families and adult adoptees, very few achieve this alternative cooperative model of intercountry adoption. A few would identify with the Moses story. Most fall somewhere in between. I don't believe this is because families didn't "do everything right." For some families there may be too many elements outside their control. Intercountry adoption is a complex experience. While I cannot control many of the factors that will contribute to my children's feelings about having been adopted, I can control some of them. Certainly, I can work to understand the role race plays in this country. I have stepped outside my comfort zone and reached out to my children's ethnic communities. This gives me the hope my children—in fact my whole family—won't be the shrimp that is crushed when two whales fight.

Putting the Kim Back on the Cake

겨울이 되어야 솔이 푸른줄 안다

We notice pine needles are green only when the winter comes.
KOREAN PROVERB

What's in a Name?

So much went into choosing our daughter's name. While waiting to adopt, I dreamed of little girls' names. In our family many of us, including myself, have the middle name Ann. I always intended if I had a daughter her middle name would be Ann. Of course, things didn't happen exactly as we expected, and Diana came to us from Korea, so we had to be creative. She had been named in Korea already. Knowing her name belonged to her as part of who she already was, we were planning to keep her Korean given name as her middle name. We began to think of names where the Ann could be incorporated into her first name. We picked her name while anxiously waiting for our referral, before we knew which child would be ours. We chose the name—Diana—Roman goddess, dressed in silver, drove the moon across the sky, protectress of women and young children. When the picture and information arrived offering us a particular child, it included her Korean name, Eun Jung, meaning in Chinese characters, "silver and pure." Clearly this was the Diana dressed in silver we were waiting for. The goddess Diana is also associated with the hunt, and as such is always surrounded by animals. My husband and I continued to enjoy the connection between Diana's names as she developed an obsession with animals. We were delighted with the "fit."

I have noticed most adoptive parents have a story romanticizing their connection to their child. My husband and I are no different. I believe it is part of the bonding process. Our bonding story for our daughter happens to be around her name. In fact, in all new relationships we look for commonality, things that show our connection. I do not share this story because I believe the fit of her name was a sign this was the child we were meant to have. As we waited for referral of a second child from Korea, which came slowly because of the Seoul Olympics, we looked through books of waiting children. One little boy in Latin America had the name Victor Emanuel, which it happens is my great grandfather's name. Had we adopted him, the name would have become significant. Since we didn't, it is a passing memory. This doesn't diminish the fact that the names Diana and Eun Jung fitting so well together is part of the bond between us, because she did become our daughter and the intertwining of our lives did become our destiny. So far, I have only talked about names from my perspective as an adoptive mother. Diana's perspective is different.

Names have also been important to Diana. In Korean school she learned to write her Korean name, Eun Jung, in *hangul*. When she was in fourth grade, we had to explain to her teacher what it was she was writing on top of all her school papers. She wrote her entire name as she knew it, Diana Eun Jung Lee Winston, with the Eun Jung in *hangul*.

Diana's name as it appeared on her fourth grade papers.

Prior to the time she came to us, Diana had lived with her birth family, and then another Korean family as their daughter, and so she claims two Korean last names. When Diana was in fourth grade we didn't yet know about the Kim, her last name from her birth family. From Diana's perspective her names were her history, and in fourth grade she made sure none of them were left out. It bothered her one was missing. Her story was incomplete.

A Dream

Diana's feelings in fourth grade were pretty normal, and whether she loved us or hated us, she was pretty good at expressing her feelings in her writing. In fifth grade, the intensity of her feelings grew beyond her ability to pen them in her journal. She found herself struggling in school, and we found her stuck in one place emotionally. She wanted to know where her birthmother was. There were many incidents connected to this emotional turmoil, but I'll share a culminating and representative one.

One evening she fell asleep early on my bed, and as I was trying to wake her up to put her in her bed, in a state between wakefulness and sleep, she asked, "Where is my mother?"

"I am right here, Diana."

"No, where is my mother?"

"I am right here."

"No, you are Chris Winston. Where is my mother?!"

Schoolwork was an impossibility. She went from succeeding to failing. We decided to find her birth family if it was possible.

Searching for My Daughter's Birth Family

In 1999, I traveled to Korea to reinforce connections for Friends of Korea and the Korean American Adoptee Adoptive Family Network. While appearing on the Korean Broadcast System Achimadang Show in Seoul, I was suddenly given the opportunity to look for my children's birth families. I took them up on it. Before I was off the air, the Lee family had called, and our connection to Diana's birth family was established.

I traveled to my daughter's hometown. It took all day to wade through the series of people connecting me to Diana's birth family. I met members of the Lee family, Mr. Kim, who was my daughter's birthfather, Diana's youngest birth sister and finally, in the twilight zone of shock and unreality, I met a woman wearing my daughter's face, who looked like a ghost. I only met with her birthmother for about ten minutes, but for all of us the shock of the meeting was overwhelming. I was thankful my daughter was safely at home in California, because while I was in very good control while meeting Diana's birth family, on the train back to Pusan where I was staying I did nothing but drip tears. Diana's birth parents were no longer a fantasy. They were real.

Meeting my daughter's birth family was a profound and life-altering event I never expected to happen. Her story came to us in bits and pieces, from different perspectives, making more of a mosaic with all the cracks between than a complete picture. The story told to us by the agency contained elements of truth, but it was incomplete and differed factually from other versions we came to hear. On one element all accounts agreed; our daughter was somehow placed in the care of a Mr. Lee and his wife by someone in her birth family before the agency became involved. The agency version, the Lee family version, and her birth family's version were all different in many sometimes troubling aspects. Some of the stories involved extreme child endangerment, and some reflected only love, but digesting these stories was difficult for me and for our daughter.

Managing My Feelings

One of the first things my daughter's birthfather told me was, "Every time I tried to get her back, they moved her." I thought back to our adoption referral papers. When we first read them years before, my husband and I had hoped the fact the paperwork documented she had lived in several locations during her first year of life wouldn't be too detrimental to her development. Those papers also stated that Diana's birth family couldn't be found. What Diana's birthfather was telling me, added a new twist to the story. If her birth family couldn't be found, how would her birthfather know she had been moved around? Certainly he had never read our referral papers.

I didn't know what to do with this information, let alone the sheer reality of her birth family's existence. I did know I needed to put my feelings together pretty quickly. I had found her birth family to help my daughter resolve her feelings, and I needed to be there for her. I had long conversations with my mother while still in Korea. I wrote fantasy descriptions of my daughter's story—fairytales, trying to come to some resolution. We had wanted to find her truth, and there seemed to be so many truths in conflict with each other, all of which belonged to Diana and not to me.

Diana Meets Her Birth Family

When Diana and her birth family started corresponding, the letters were beautiful. No one in such a circumstance could have written better. We were lucky Eyoungsoo agreed to be our translator. Not only did we have someone bicultural who could understand both Korean and American sensibilities, but he was also a psychologist. We had the best guidance. My daughter wrote back, and it was fascinating to see what they shared. She and her birth family corresponded for nine months. My daughter told me she wanted them to write to her, but she never wanted to meet them. I believed such a decision was entirely hers to make. So, you can imagine my surprise when we were given an opportunity to visit Korea, and my daughter expressed the desire to meet her birth family. With my daughter, then twelve, I traveled by plane and then by train to her hometown.

She comes from an otherwise intact family and is the youngest of three daughters. She has sisters who are five years older and eleven months older than Diana. Before the reconnection, her sisters did not know of her existence. Things did not become settled right away. Diana, her birth family, and her adoptive family were rafting on a roiling river of emotion, coming to terms with her real story. It was *hard* work for all of us, most especially for her. After about a year, her thinking became settled, and the girl who was stuck, began to pull things together at school and to have a better sense of who she was. She found out her birth name was Kim, but she was keeping the Lee too. She found her history in all of her names. During that time of emotional processing while corresponding with her birth family, my daughter still had many questions without answers. The only truth I think we confirmed was my daughter does have two families. If you count the Lee family, she has three families.

After arriving early in the evening in her hometown, we called to confirm with her birthfather the plans for meeting the next day. He wanted to come to our hotel immediately, saying he had been waiting not only all day, but years, to see his daughter. My daughter was uncomfortable. She had made a careful and, for her, comfortable plan for meeting her birth family, and he was altering the script. He came, but honoring my daughter's wishes, only I met him in the lobby of the hotel with my friend who came to translate for us. The meeting was different this time. Though we had only met once before, we hugged each other. It was a good thing because we talked very openly of how to meet the needs of my daughter, his wife, and his other daughters. I tactfully explained why my daughter could not meet him that evening.

"She is shy," I said.

"Yes, I understand," her birthfather said. "All of my girls are like that."

We met the next morning. My daughter and I walked down to the lobby where her birthmother, birthfather, and sisters were waiting. My daughter bowed and said, "*Anyunghaseo* (Hello)" as she gave them each a small gift with two hands. Her birthmother held my daughter's hand as they walked, until they both drifted away from the intensity of it. We had *galbi* (beef short ribs with Korean barbecue sauce) for lunch, my daughter's favorite. We walked through town shopping, and my daughter and her sisters had their picture

Diana (center) with her two older sisters in Korea.

taken in funny wigs in a photo shop. When her sisters got too far ahead, my daughter called out, "*Unie*" (big sister), to have them wait for her. They had fun. Then, her father took us to an island with a zoo, amusement park, and arcade. He had chosen the zoo because my daughter, like her birth family, really adores animals. I was deeply impressed with how her birthfather gave

my daughter space, and yet was always close enough for interaction. He ended up teaching her to shoot arrows in the arcade.

This day belonged to Diana, but I was essential for her sense of security. I found a good role for myself, documenting the day's events with a camera. I was grateful my daughter can speak a little Korean. I was grateful it was not her first trip to Korea. I was so glad we had participated in the Friends of Korea Family

Mark welcomes us home from the trip to meet Diana's birth family.

Exchange Program, and she had had other experiences communicating with and building relationships with other kids her age who don't speak English. It is incredible having shared this experience with my daughter.

Since the one time they met, Diana has not wanted to meet with her birth family again, though she has been back to Korea. In fact it mattered a lot to her that she could go back to Korea without seeing her birth family. She thinks of being in Korea and being with her birth family as separate events. Her birth family has seemed cautious about meeting her again, as well. Over time the lack of comfort level between Diana and her birth family seems to have increased rather than decreased, which has surprised me. This decrease in comfort level seems to have more to do with family values than it has to do with cultural difference or the reason for the adoption. At this point in time, it is the difference in family values that has become most difficult for Diana to manage.

Whatever ideas I have about how their interactions should be and how often they occur, I keep to myself. It is her relationship and not mine. Correspondence has tapered off, though Diana has responded to every letter sent to her by her birth family. The difficulty in corresponding seems to be mutual. She thought she might write to them when she graduated from high school, but decided not to. It was up to her. I feel the reality of her high school graduation was in part due to her having met her birth family. Her mind became more settled after she met them, and all the events in her life were less volatile. From the time she met them, she had only her actual story to process, rather than endless fantasy stories spinning in her head.

Some Adoptees Connect Closely with Birth Family

Camille Beck met her birth family around the same age and time Diana met hers. She also comes from an otherwise intact family that includes not only two older birth sisters, but also a younger brother. Despite that similarity, Camille's relationship with her birth family has developed much differently than Diana's has. She has already visited her birth family three times in Korea. Her entire birth family visited her following her high school graduation. She says, "I enjoyed visiting them in Korea, seeing how they lived their everyday life. I enjoyed being part of such a big family. That was the best part for me because we don't live close to either my mom's or my dad's family here in Seattle. I enjoyed them visiting me because I was able to show them where I have grown up, what I do, and where I go to school."

I asked Camille what the single most enjoyable experience was for her in visiting her birth family. She told me it was when she went off shopping with her siblings. They went to whichever stores they wanted and spent all their money. Who wouldn't enjoy that? It was similar to what Diana enjoyed most the time she met her sisters in Korea.

Camille also appreciates that her adoptive parents are comfortable with her birth parents. When I asked Camille how she knows her adoptive parents are comfortable with her birth family, she answered, "Because when we visit Korea, my parents allow me to sleep at my birth parents' house and be alone with them. My parents have welcomed my birth family to our house and act as friends to them. My mom said, 'They are the easiest people to get along with.' I have a bunch of pictures hanging in my room of my birth family, and my parents are not offended by this."

Camille offered to write a short piece for me about why she herself feels comfortable with her birth family. She sent me the following:

> I find a certain comfort in my birth family. One reason is my birth family has a lifestyle that is very similar to mine. I was raised with parents who care a lot about me and protect me. Similarly, my birth family has a lot of the same educational and lifelong expectations of my siblings. Because my sisters and I have similar lifestyles and are close in age, we get along well and understand each other. Without words, my birthmom, sisters, and I respond with similar emotions in many situations.

My relationships with my brother and father are as meaningful as my relationships with my sisters and mom. My father is a man on the go, who likes to be independent and likes to learn new things; I've noticed these same traits in my brother. Both of them point to show me something new, important, or interesting so that they can communicate with me without really having to talk. My brother and I have always had trouble communicating because of the language barrier, but we are now both learning more of each other's languages. We are trying to communicate more, and I really appreciate his efforts.

Diana has not attained the same comfort level with her birth family that Camille has with hers. The task fell to Diana's oldest birth sister to be the correspondent with Diana for the entire birth family. This oldest sister is now married with two kids of her own. She is busy with her family and doesn't speak English. No one in Diana's birth family speaks English or has email access. The education level is also different, Diana being the only one

Camille (second from left) with her birth family.

among her siblings in Korea and birth parents to go beyond middle school. For now, the educational and economic difference feels like a bigger wall to overcome than the cultural one in building relationships. I don't know if it will be that way in the future.

The empathy I feel for the grief Diana's birth family must feel in not hearing from her, is tempered by the fact Diana's needs are first and foremost for me. I feel sad for Diana that her birth family had difficulty in writing to her more often. On the other hand, Diana has more than many adoptees have in being acknowledged by birth family and in getting the answers she wanted. One thing I do know is I trust Diana to know what her needs are. When and if she needs to contact her birth family again, she will. I take comfort in the fact we have no plans to leave this house where our children grew up. Our phone number will remain the same. Though her birth family may move, we will not. I have sometimes had the fantasy of developing a relationship with Diana's birth family myself, so they could know how she is doing. However, it is not my place to do so. I would not correspond with my daughter's birth family on my own, unless that were Diana's wish. It is her connection and not mine. What I can do is to make sure the opportunity for reconnection remains unbroken if they need each other in the future. Pine needles are green all year long, even if we only notice them in the winter.

A Moment in Time

At the time we found Diana's birth parents, they were still living in the same neighborhood where Diana was born, though in a different location. The Lee family saw me on KBS and called in, saying they knew Diana's birth parents. At that time, I was accompanied by Eyoungsoo. When Eyoungsoo talked with them, they told him they didn't know the names of Diana's birth parents and were not sure exactly where they were living, however, they knew the neighborhood and would go there and walk around. In walking around, they felt sure they could find them. They did.

Within sight of where Diana's birth family was living, was the house where Diana had been born, and the first orphanage she was in. Both buildings were condemned, but Diana's birthfather broke the locks off, and we took pictures. Today those buildings no longer stand. Diana's birth family has moved due to a typhoon. I am glad she has the pictures.

Were Diana to go on TV in Korea today, it is likely the connection could no longer be made. I don't believe her birth parents could have overcome their feelings of guilt to make the phone call. Since they have moved, it is doubtful the Lee family could have found them. As her mother, I am very glad we were able to find Diana's birth family at that time. She made the most of the opportunity in terms of using the experience to answer questions that mattered to her. While Diana may not have the same level of relationship as Camille, she has more answers than David.

In writing this I asked Diana, now eighteen, "Do you ever wish you hadn't met your birth parents?"

"Yeah, sometimes," she said, "when I feel guilty for not writing to them."

"Are there any reasons you are glad you met them?"

"I am glad to know they are alive. I am glad I got to know who they are. I am glad I got to finally be able to figure out what I think is the truth."

"Do you wish you had waited until now that you are eighteen to find them?"

"No, I am glad I met them when I really cared about finding them, when I wanted to know the truth."

Birth Parents Perspective

Over the years in taking families to Korea with the Friends of Korea Family Exchange Program, I have had the opportunity to assist Eyoungsoo in facilitating other birth parent and adoptee meetings. It has been a privilege whenever I have had that opportunity. Each reunion has been different.

In spite of the language and cultural barrier, I have had the opportunity to meet a variety of people in various situations.

In one case I was there when an adoptee met a birthmother who didn't want to meet her. She only did so grudgingly as a one-time event. She was not receptive to any questions. While one could understand her concerns for anonymity, it was clear there were many feelings under the surface. The birthmother's relationship to the birthfather was not something she wanted to remember. She advised the adoptee to go on with her life and not to contact her again. The adoptee left with some questions answered and others unanswered.

In another case I was there when an adoptee, the son of a close friend, met birth parents who had been told he had died at birth. He was placed for adoption by his grandmother, who did not want his birth parents to marry. They married any way. From the time they knew of his existence, his birth parents had been longing to meet him. At the actual meeting, emotions were high. To this date the relationship has continued.

In yet another case, I was called by a Korean American who is a pastor here in the United States. He was friends with a pastor in Korea. The pastor in Korea had two members of his congregation who had recently passed away. They had placed their only child, a daughter, for adoption when they had to enter a leper colony. In their will they left her property in Seoul. The pastor had the last name and initial geographical location of the adoptive family at the time of adoption. The adoptive family had an uncommon last name. Amazingly there was only one listing for that name in the city when I called directory assistance. The adoptee's family had moved, but it was her great aunt. I understand the adoptee did make the connection.

This leads me to the conclusion that, while their stories may have some commonality, birth parents are as individual as adoptees and adoptive parents. None of us can speak for the others. When birth parents remain as fantasies, the humanity and the uniqueness of each birth parent can be lost. It is my hope Korean birth parents, over time, will have more opportunities to speak for themselves. They deserve to be more than two-dimensional, cardboard people.

Recently, I was given a gift of seeing search and reunion more closely through a birthfather's eyes. A Korean American man came forward, offering support to KAAN. After some time of our getting to know him, he finally shared that he was a birthfather. He wanted help to find his daughter who was living with her adoptive family in the United States. He had obtained some limited information about her from the adoption agency in Korea. He knew her American name, her approximate geographical location, that she had graduated from high school, her occupation, and that she was getting married in the summer.

Using the KAAN network, we reached out to someone in her geographic location. Through wedding registries and classmates.com, we were able to make her general geographic location more exact. With the name of the particular suburb, we were able to find an adoptive family who knew the adoptee. In fact, she was their babysitter.

For the first time, I was involved in a meeting initiated by the birth parent rather than the adoptee. It was my first opportunity to know a birth parent well enough to be able to come close to experiencing search through his eyes. His perspective appeared different than I had anticipated. While he was concerned that she was okay and had been raised well, that didn't appear to be the focus of his emotional turmoil and confusion. He had found his baby girl, but she was twenty-one years old. It seemed a struggle for him to process that fact. He seemed much more concerned about whether he could reclaim a relationship with her than he was in hearing about her adoptive parents. Though language was still an issue, having lived in the United States, he had some English. I was more able to communicate with him than I had been with birth parents in my previous experiences.

Feeling the birth parents made a plan for their baby's adoption, adoptive parents hope to show the birth parents that the trust placed in the adoptive parents was warranted. Many times in first meetings, a photo album comes out to show what a good life the adoptee has had. This adoptee had such an album. This birthfather on hearing repeatedly what a good life the adoptee had led and how happy she was with her adoptive family, said to us when she was no longer present, "They have given her everything. There is no place for me." I realized the loss involved in the presentation of that photo album. Sharing a photo album doesn't seem a bad impulse and does provide a focus for sharing at first meeting, but how it is handled may be important. Even sharing good things can cause birth parents to experience grief.

Over the years prior to meeting my daughter's birth parents, I had thoughts of them almost as my brother and sister, joined by our common child. My impulse was to thank them for the opportunity they gave me to be a parent. Yet, in the case of Diana's birth parents, they didn't intend to place their daughter in an overseas adoption at all. Knowing they would have preferred to raise Diana themselves, "thanks" doesn't seem like what they would want to hear. How can you thank someone for something they did not wish to give? I wonder how Diana's birth family felt about the photo album that we gave them. I imagine that they were glad that she had been well taken care of, but it must have been so bittersweet. In the two meetings I had with them, I developed a respect for them as Diana's birth parents, a respect for their feelings, and a wish for their well-being. My impression was they felt the same way about me. I hope that in my limited interactions with them, I have shown less concern about my needs and more of a respect for their needs. I was the one who gained what they lost.

Whose Relationship Is It?

I am well aware it has become controversial for minor Korean adoptees to meet their birth families. On some levels I understand and agree with those who warn against it. It is not for everyone. It can be an intense experience, difficult to manage without preparation. One never knows what truths one will find. Most importantly, search and reunion belong, after all, to adoptees themselves and their birth parents. It is very easy for adoptive parents of younger children to usurp the relationship with birth parents, and, frankly, it can be quite tempting to do so.

In the beginning I had sporadic impulses to write letters to Diana's birth parents myself, to send money to the family for Diana's sisters' education, to become more involved. I could see Diana's sisters weren't likely to receive the same education she would, and it might be a wall between them, as indeed it appears to be. Yet, who was I to make judgments about them? Could I accept them as they were without trying to change them? Every time I had those impulses, Diana let me know quite clearly she didn't like it. Eyoungsoo was squarely on Diana's side. "Diana is in the driver's seat," he said. "Give her the steering wheel." I thank him for his stubbornness and persistence about that, because he was right. I realize how I could have gotten in the way. She has her birth parents' address and they have hers. They can write if they want to or need to. They are reconnected now, the relationship belongs to them to develop, or not, as they choose. I will be here to support Diana in whatever way she desires.

Putting the Kim Back on the Cake

Because of meeting her birth family, Diana had a chance to reclaim her history. On Diana's thirteenth birthday, her actual birthday which was not the same date as on her adoption paperwork and so not her legal birthday, we bought a birthday cake for her. It was her first birthday after meeting her birth family. My husband went to order the cake, and he asked them to write "Happy Birthday Diana Eun Jung Kim Lee Winston" on it. Somehow the bakery managed to leave out the Kim. We knew we had to fix it. So Elaine, my oldest son's fiancée now wife, went and picked up some decorative frosting. She set to work, putting the Kim back on the cake. It was symbolic of the task Diana, and indeed all of us, had undertaken. With the Kim back on the cake, Diana's past belongs to her.

A Better Life

내 사는 곳이 고향

Wherever you live is your hometown.
KOREAN PROVERB

Meeting Gwang Moon

On November 30, 2002, I was given the wonderful opportunity of meeting a young man who had grown up in a Korean orphanage and was willing to share his story. Gwang Moon Na did so readily. Gwang Moon and my son, whose Korean name is Sang Moon, share part of their name in the way Korean brothers share a name. They also share having spent time in a Korean orphanage—my son only for two and a half years, Gwang Moon for much longer. They are not brothers by birth or adoption and have never met each other. But, there is something about both of them that is enticing, something that reminds me each of the other.

I think the thing linking them in my mind is a sense they have a core of steel, some inner strength you don't mess with. I was drawn to Gwang Moon. He told me that many years ago, when he was nine years old, he

Gwang Moon Na and
David Sang Moon Winston in 2002.

had a possibility of being adopted in Switzerland. He said I reminded him of his Swiss sponsor. She was sponsoring several children from Gongsaengwon Orphanage at the time and chose one of the others to adopt, perhaps because Gwang Moon came as a package with his older brother and sister. He told me he does sometimes wonder how his life might have been different had he been adopted, but he does not romanticize.

He said, "I might have had a lot of conflicts and troubles adjusting to the language and culture."

He said the adoptees from Europe he has met seemed confused. He wondered if he would have been that way. Yet he really felt that if that had been his life, he would have made the best of it. Adoption is not something he longed for or wishes had been. He is intelligent and thoughtful enough to know it would have been challenging in its own way.

Somehow I have the feeling he would have made the best of what life offered him, either in Korea or in Switzerland. While talking with him, I had the compelling feeling to tell him that had I met him when he was nine years old, I would have wanted to adopt him. When it was translated to him, he misunderstood. "No, no, no, no," he said. "No, not now, when you were nine," I replied. Now, I realize the inappropriateness of my remarks to him. He didn't want to be rescued. My comments were really about working out issues within myself and had nothing to do with him. He is content with his life. It made me think about all who work in adoption agencies and/or who are adoptive parents, who feel a tinge of righteousness for "rescuing" kids from orphanages.

My son, Sang Moon, has the same compelling, intelligent, spine-of-steel quality that I saw again in Gwang Moon. That survivor skill challenged us quite a bit in the beginning. Our son had a difficult adjustment to our family and to the United States. Learning English was something he wanted to avoid. Several years later, despite his clear intelligence, his report card in sixth grade was abysmal. It didn't stay that way, yet struggles with written English persisted into high school. We went through a lot while connecting as family. Yet, we did connect. Still he often challenged me about our adoption of him. I remember the following conversation with him when he was around the age of twelve and was dealing with racism at school.

As he pestered me, I asked him, "Do you think Caucasian parents should be adopting Asian children?"

"Didn't you think about racism?!" he shouted back.

"I didn't know how to think about racism, David. I have always been in situations where my ethnicity was the majority. Would you like to move into Sacramento where there are more Asians?"

"It wouldn't help, Mom. *You'd* still be white."

As with Gwang Moon, I have the feeling Sang Moon would have made the best of what life offered him, even had he stayed in Korea. He voiced this once to a reporter at the first KAAN conference when he was fourteen.

He said, "If I had stayed in Korea, it might have been better, or it might have been worse, but this is my life. I've got new parents now."

He takes what life has to offer and makes the best of it. Like Gwang Moon, he does not want to be rescued—loved and understood, perhaps, but not rescued.

Gwang Moon's Life in His Own Words

Gwang Moon Na wrote his life story in Korean. It is printed here with his permission. It was translated into English by Da Hee Son of InKAS

I was born as the youngest of three children in a small fishing village. My mother, having suffered too much from poverty and my father's mental illness, ran away. I remember making a big fuss asking my grandmother to breastfeed me when I was four. When I was six years old, we had my grandmother's funeral. Knowing my father was unable to take care of my siblings and me, my mother sneaked into our house one day and took us to our uncle. After my father came looking for us at our uncle's home, we had to leave. My mother made a desperate effort to support us, but it was too much for her to take all the responsibilities. She finally asked her grandfather's sister to take us to an orphanage. That was when I was in grade two.

I started to learn how to live in an orphanage, but it was hard. Older kids from the orphanage constantly beat me up. These horrible experiences caused me to run away from the orphanage three times, creating personal problems for me. I had difficulty building personal relationships and was always wearing a worried look on my face. I didn't have money to buy school supplies, whereas other kids didn't have to worry about that. My self-esteem fell lower. On Korean Thanksgiving Day, when I was in grade six, my mother made a visit to the orphanage to see my brother, sister, and me. I had such enormous anger toward her; I ran from her sight.

I remember I spent many sleepless nights worrying to death about getting art supplies when I was in junior high. It continuously floated around in my head that it would be so much different if I lived with parents. I entered a commercial high school since I had no interest in academic studies. Soon after I got into the school, I started sleeping over at a friend's house because I hated going to the orphanage. I was in the school rock band and typically started drinking and smoking. I was sinking into all sorts of social vice. My grades that used to be high in grade ten were gradually dropping. The teachers worried and scolded me. Once when I was in grade twelve, I stayed in school late practicing for the concert and fell asleep at school. When my homeroom teacher found out, he stormed at me for staying overnight in school. His scolding was eventually focused on the cause of the dramatic fall of my grades.

Completely unexpectedly, I got accepted into a local public university. It was after I entered the university that I started having symptoms of mental problems. Suffering from insomnia, I used to stay up all night and just managed to get to sleep by 7:00 the next morning. Having severe anxiety attacks, I began to take tranquilizers. I eventually had to quit school. I felt really sorry to the director of our orphanage, who had helped me.

I asked the pastor, who is the son of the director of our orphanage, for help to treat my mental illness. I was tempted to commit suicide so many times in the past. Now, looking back on those days, I do feel God was guiding me and protecting me from the temptation of suicide. After I received Jesus Christ in me and tried to live in his words and prayers for a year, a miracle happened: My mental illness disappeared. I was so grateful to God. Living as a new-born Christian, I got a call from a mental institute one day. I heard my father was in critical condition in a hospital and needed a caretaker. My father, whom I had never called a father since I was young, was waiting for me in the Intensive Care Unit in a hospital. It had been seventeen years. He was lying there like that. I was speechless. It was too challenging for me to accept that this man lying there helplessly was my father. While I took care of him in the hospital, what really comforted me was this thought, "I have so many friends in our orphanage who have never met their fathers. Compared to them I am a happy person." I really tried my best to take care of my father. He passed away six months later. That was a hard time, but it made me mature mentally and spiritually.

Currently I am working in Mokpo Nursing Home for the Severely Handicapped. My girlfriend also works there. At the same time I am attending a night college for my future. When I'm off work, I help my mother who's running a small restaurant. I thank God for my life as an orphan. It has given me the insight I will need to be a therapist for people with mental illness and for orphans. I work hard today, so that potentially I may be a pastor in the future.

Korean Children in Need of Social Welfare Services

At one time there existed a universal set of children needing social welfare services in Korea. At Gongsaengwon I learned that among themselves, kids in the orphanage in Korea have already divided themselves into subsets. There are "real orphans," "half orphans," and "false orphans." In other words, some have contact with birth family to varying degrees and some don't. Most are from poor families. Sometimes, though, regardless of income level, kids are in an orphanage because of having divorced and remarried parents, single mothers, or physical or mental handicaps.

Among adult Korean American adoptees there are also subsets. They were adopted at different ages. Some have contact with birth family, and some don't. They come from the same variety of background circumstances as the kids who were raised in orphanages in Korea. Some have had exposure and connection to other adoptees, and some haven't. Some have had connection to their Korean heritage and fellow Asian Americans, and some haven't. Some have had wonderful experiences in their adoptive families, and for some it has been a nightmare. Some continue to have good relationships with adoptive families, and some don't. All have been raised in a country other than Korea.

It is not my intent to glorify life in an orphanage or the life of poor or broken families anywhere in the world. When you read Gwang Moon's story, you see he has not had an easy time. If you lived in our house for the first six years our son, Sang Moon, was with us, you might also feel he did not have an easy time. Yet, both Sang Moon and Gwang Moon are accepting of what life has brought to them. Both of them have similar goals, sharing an interest in psychology. Of course, I know we could just as easily find both someone who was raised in a Korean orphanage and an adoptee who have not found happiness or acceptance in their lives, because the challenges they have faced were simply too overwhelming. The point is no one can know whether staying in one's native country, even while living in an orphanage, or going overseas for adoption, will result in the greatest happiness for any particular individual. There is too much diversity among orphans in Korea and adoptees in America to answer the question. In addition to all the other factors causing diversity in our original universal set of children needing social services in Korea, we have the inherent uniqueness of each individual and their differing reactions to life's circumstances.

Another Example

One of my best friends is a Korean American psychologist in his mid-sixties, too old to have been a candidate for the adoption system in Korea. He was one of eight children raised by his single illiterate mother in Korea after his father died when he was five. During the Japanese occupation they ate tree bark, grasshoppers, grass, and millet. He had one outfit he wore, and he told me the sleeves got shiny from wiping away snot from numerous colds in the winter when he was a little boy. Two of his siblings died of infectious diseases. One night just prior to the Korean War, when he was nine, he was walking home from a school meeting with his ten-year-old brother and two other boys from their village. They were shot at by soldiers. His brother and one of the other boys were killed in front of him before he ran for his life.

Yet, he says to me, "I am so grateful no one ever told me I was poor. I wonder how it would have been had someone come in, taken the struggle away from me, and rescued me. Who would I be?"

Instead, he eventually found a way to get himself into Seoul National University before making his own decision to immigrate. He is one of the strongest people I know, and I believe his strength comes from his ownership of his own survival. Yet, it seems to me many people, and perhaps countries, have their strength sapped when they are in the position of needing to be rescued.

"A Better Life"

Once during the time my daughter was adjusting to the finding of her birth family, she made the statement that by allowing her to be adopted, her birth family had ruined her life.

I asked her, "Did they really make it worse, or better?"

Her answer was, "Both."

In the beginning, having been given the awesome responsibility of raising someone else's child as my own, I had a strong need to believe in the rightness of what I was doing. I did believe that by adopting my children I was giving them a better life. It kept me from being wrong about wanting to be a mother so much. It kept me from feeling too sad that my gain might be someone else's loss. But, what does "better" mean? "Better" implies an alternative between two choices. Life is not static. There are many times when our lives branch and go in unexpected directions; making a comparison with what might have been is difficult. Usually a better life seems to mean educational and economic opportunities. What happens when because of reasons of emotional or intellectual limits, or because of personal choice, adoptees do not take advantage of those opportunities? Have we given them a better life? Must they succeed to prove us right? Or can it be more about their own individual struggles as human beings? I do believe the onus of adoptive parents needing to provide and adoptees needing to succeed sits heavily on the relationship. Happiness and being better off are very subjective things.

Someone once said to me, "Had your daughter stayed in Korea, the best she could have been was a vendor in a market."

Given the love her married birth parents show her two sisters despite their economic challenges, and the endless garage sales our daughter loves to hold in our driveway, would that have been such a bad thing?

"Giving Back"

It is for all the reasons I have stated that both adoption agencies and adoptive parents would do well to avoid a rescue fantasy and approach their role with humility. Evaluating my role in the adoption of my children is not about feeling guilty or wrong, but about accepting my own humanity. The children who left Korea and joined adoptive families in other countries did not do so by their own choice. Adoptive parents wanted them and adoption agencies in Korea were placing them as the primary means of dealing with the children needing social services in Korea.

Unquestionably, in many cases, perhaps most cases, adoptive parents and adoptees have entered into a relationship bringing joy and love to each. The value of Sang Moon's and our family's adoption experience is not derived from the computer in his room, the college education we can fund for him, or his red Toyota Camry in the driveway. Instead, we find meaning in the struggle we have walked through to come together as family. The significance is in our admiration of his ability never to give up and to keep on striving. It is also in his appreciation for our continued efforts at understanding. Together it is this bond that makes our experience meaningful.

A relationship is not well founded when one individual in the relationship is always seen as the giver and the other is always the recipient who is expected to be grateful. The expectation of gratitude gets in the way of relationship. In a parent-child relationship, the parent gains as much or more in personal growth as does the child. Relationships work best when both parties benefit. So I wonder about those people who sometimes express the feeling that adoptees need to "give something back." Why adoptees? Is it for being rescued? Who decides they have been rescued? To whom are they owing? They have no reason to feel a need to "give back" any more than anyone else in this life.

Rescued victims expected to pay back are not the ones who have the most to give. The joy of community service, of making a difference in the world, is felt by every human being regardless of his circumstance when he feels something within himself is meaningful to others. It is those who from the strength within themselves find something valuable to give who gain from giving back. Perhaps part of Gwang Moon's motivation to become a pastor is to help others as he has been helped. My feeling is it is more that his life experience has strengthened him, giving him something of value he can be proud to share with others. For both Gwang Moon and Sang Moon, "giving back" is a demonstration of their strength and not their weakness, the timing of which is theirs to decide and should not be expected of them. "Giving back" is, as the word "giving" implies, a gift.

Feelings About Adoption

I believe in interethnic relationships, and I believe in adoption, knowing full well the outcome for any particular child, placed even in the best of circumstances, will remain unknown, clouded until the future arrives. As adoptive parents, we don't have to justify the validity of our experience. We do not have to prove our children are better off with us than they might have been somewhere else. To think that way, I feel, is a detriment to a good relationship. It has helped me that whenever I have had thoughts about my own children's probable fates had I not adopted them, that I have not stayed in that space. I don't apologize for adopting my kids, because I am not all knowing. I adopted them because I wanted more kids, they were available, and it seemed right. I do my best to give them the brightest lives I can. I feel lucky to have them, and I value our relationships.

Living with Boundries

아는 길도 물어 가라

Even though you know the way, ask.
KOREAN PROVERB

Acknowledging Differences

After the birth of my oldest son, Alexis, my father-in-law made the comment, "He is the first Winston in seven generations to be born outside of Texas." We had moved to California because my husband wanted to work for Intel. We went on to add two additional Winstons to our family, born not only outside of Texas, but also outside of the United States. We were choosing to do something different.

My husband's parents and my parents have always been very loving and accepting of all our children. Pictures of all three are displayed in their houses in Texas and Michigan. All have received the same gifts, love, and recognition. Surely there was loss for our parents, not only because their grandchildren were not born in Texas, but because we moved so far away to raise them. We have received love and acceptance, but we are different. Our family is composed of genetic Winstons, my husband and my oldest son, and three not genetic Winstons, myself and David and Diana. Of course Alexis and I share Hubbard genetics. Mark, David, and Diana do not. David and Diana each have their own individual well of genetic possibilities. We can divide ourselves by gender as well, three male Winstons and two female Winstons. Two of us are Asian, and three of us are Caucasian.

Differences are to be expected within a family, including differences in personality. On the positive side, the differences we bring and share with each other enrich our lives. I expected such enrichment from the adoption of my children, and I have found it. But, the enrichment didn't occur only in the way I expected. For me, adoption turned out to be more than a chance to broaden my view by learning about and visiting another country. While my children primarily wanted to be loved and enjoyed, the differences interethnic adoption brought to our family were sometimes heavier than we had anticipated. All three of my children were visibly different for the whole world to see.

My son, Alexis, described how the visible difference in our family affected him when in his essay for college admission he wrote:

> After being an only child for nine years, I adopted a little sister (from Korea). Our trip to pick her up was my first time outside the country, other than Canada. Korea was very different. This event affected me deeply, as did our return two years later to get my brother, David. However the most important part of this experience came later, after we were home.
>
> I was always different from other children my age. I was teased mercilessly in elementary school. But, never before had grown adults stared openly at my family, or acted surprised when I introduced my brother as my brother. The incidents, though few, have had a lasting effect. There are good aspects of my siblings' ethnicity. My mother became involved in the Korean American Community in Sacramento. Through her, so did I. My experiences with

people from other cultures gave me a new perspective. I learned the differences in individual personality are more important than cultural differences."

Feeling different can sometimes be an exhilarating experience, especially when we make the choice to be different. When we are not the ones who made the choice to be different, difference is not always comfortable. The enrichment that occurred in our family came when we did the emotional work of untangling the challenges inherent in the unique life experience of being an interethnic family formed through adoption. Our relationships were enhanced when our family acknowledged that those differences brought boundaries. We became closer to each other when we found the balance in how to define, respect, or ignore those boundaries.

Boundaries and "Things Korean"

One adult adoptee I met told me she so wished her mother cared about Korea in the way this adoptee saw me caring about it. She said her mother had no interest in Korea at all. When she said her mother had no interest in Korea, it sounded as if she was saying, "My mother has no deep interest in me." When an opportunity arose for us to travel to her motherland, this adoptee and her mother joined the group. Listening to her daughter, the mother began to learn more about her daughter's birth heritage. In fact she became genuinely very interested in Korea and began to learn the language. Suddenly this adoptee friend was complaining that her mother was continuously practicing Korean. If connection to Korea belongs to adoptees, do adoptive parents usurp that when they make the connection their own? At first this adoptee's mother didn't make much connection to Korea, acting as if doing so was almost a chore. The mother was only connecting to Korean heritage when she felt she had to for her daughter's well-being. Because the adoptee saw her birth heritage as an integral part of herself, she felt her mother did not value something inherent in her makeup. She felt less loved. She wanted her mother to genuinely love Korea, but she didn't want her mother to take over Korea. They had difficulty finding the balance, but they were trying.

It is work to define boundaries, because they are fluid, forming uniquely at various times in different spaces. I developed my own links to Korea, in support of my children's need for connection. I enjoyed connecting in the same way I enjoyed my children, making friendships, learning and growing in a host of ways. It has sometimes been difficult for me to figure out where I "fit." Occasionally, with groups of Korean American friends, I have been called "honorary Korean" or "volunteer Korean," even "blonde Korean." I always appreciate the love expressed in these words of inclusion. Yet, I know I am not any sort of Korean at all. On the other hand, because of the way our family was formed, my connection to Korea is deeper than that of other Euro-Americans. I want to be included in an appropriate way.

Not too long ago, I was fortunate to have success in dieting, dropping quite a few pounds. Unfortunately, when I went to get ready for a Korean Community event with my Korean American friends, I found that none of my nice clothes fit.

Diana, watching me, asked, "Why don't you wear your *hanbok*?"

I told her, "I wouldn't feel comfortable wearing it by myself. If Grace Kim said, 'Everyone is wearing their *hanboks*, so wear yours,' I would. Or if you were going and wanted to wear yours and wanted me to wear it with you, I would. But, somehow, I don't want to be the only one doing it."

"Because you are only Korean because of me?" she asked.

"Right," I said. Somehow we all have to know who we are.

I felt I had a comfortable boundary about when to wear a *hanbok*, but to illustrate how boundaries are continually reevaluated, the issue arose again. We were to attend a large Korean American Community event to which my family and many other adoptive families had bought tickets. I was asked to wear my *hanbok* by Denise Park, our Friends of Korea Kid's Club teacher. Though I did not know it, my efforts in building Friends of Korea were also going to be recognized. It was clear most of the Korean Americans would not be wearing traditional Korean clothing, but the wives of a few of the organizers would be. So, I would not be following my boundary of wearing my *hanbok* when most of the Koreans were wearing theirs. Nor would I be following my boundary of my kids wanting to wear *hanboks* and my wearing mine with them.

I continue to attend these events, though my grown Korean-born children often do not, because the friendships I have made in this community are genuine. I don't want to suddenly stop attending Korean American events as if to say, "My kids are grown now. I got what I wanted from you. I am moving on." Though not Korean, I will always be a part of the Korean American Community in Sacramento.

My kids were willing to attend this particular event in support of our community as well, but they did not want to wear their *hanboks*. They have a different feeling about that now as young adults than they did as children. Because my children are now adults, my own sensitivities are also changing. I am no longer a parent building bridges for them. So, following the Korean proverb, I decided that even though I thought I knew the way, I would ask.

I asked David, "What do you think of my wearing my *hanbok*?"

"Do I have to wear one?" he asked.

"No," I said.

"Go for it, Mom," he replied.

Still somewhat uncomfortable, I put my Korean clothing on at the event and encountered another adoptive mom of a young child from Korea. The child was dressed in her *hanbok* and her eyes lit up when she saw I had one for her mother to wear. Her mother was less sure, but seeing her daughter's face, she put it on.

"It means a lot to her," I said.

"I know," she said.

Walking away from her, I ran into one of our teen dancers in Friends of Korea's Han Ma Eum Dance group. It is a group primarily composed of teenage adoptees, who were dancing for the evening's entertainment. We had a new dance teacher. The teens were excited with how authentically Korean their dancing was getting and how much their dancing had improved. Yet the old dance teacher had let them do their makeup themselves. The new teacher wanted to do their makeup, all the same, in a very Korean style. This dancer missed not doing her own makeup and was thinking about her own boundaries, American or Korean.

"Isn't it more Korean this way?" I asked her.

"Yes."

"But, you are an American girl?" I asked.

"Exactly," she said.

"So, what do you think of this white lady in the purple *hanbok*? Do you think it looks like I am trying to be Korean when I am not?" I asked her.

"I like that you are willing to be with us," she said with a smile.

"Isn't it tough working out our feelings about these things?" I asked

"Yeah," she replied.

I realized then I was wearing the *hanbok* in support of my Friends of Korea community, those adoptive families following behind me, no longer for my own children. That is where the mental struggle over boundaries had come in. What I might want to do for my own kids, and what I might want to do for Friends of Korea families were different. In this case they were not incompatible, but they could have been. If there had been adopted adult

Over the years the Winstons have had many opportunities to wear hanboks.

Koreans attending the event, especially those attending a Korean function for the first time, trying to grasp at a connection, I would have been more uncomfortable with my connection staring them in the face.

While so far wearing a *hanbok* has been the right thing to do, there are going to be times when it won't be. The decisions about boundaries are not made once, but continually. When David arrived in our family, he faced an abrupt change in language, culture, and food. I learned to cook Korean food for him, but now my daughter, Diana, can cook many more Korean dishes than I can. I ease back from that. I am not in a hurry to stand in her space.

In the early years, because making Korean connections proved a challenge, I learned Korean language at least well enough to eavesdrop. I got out my Korean dictionary and translated the weekly Sacramento page in the *Korea Times* so I could understand what was going on. It was not so difficult for me. I love language and have always wished I could speak more than one. I enjoyed studying Spanish in college, but somehow lost the time for it afterward. Learning Korean was fun. Yet, as the years went on, I studied Korean language less and less. When my children were in high school and were studying Korean as independent study to meet their high school language requirement, I stopped entirely.

It was one thing to learn Korean in support of my children, building a bridge of connections for them to walk across. It was another to be in their space and usurp their connection, particularly when learning language didn't seem to be an easy task for them. Speaking Korean better than they do, being more Korean than they are, has never been my goal. I have cared genuinely about Korea separate from my children, though, which I think is important. I wouldn't want my kids to feel that connecting to their birth heritage in support of them has been an unpleasant task I suffered only for them. Though my experiences have sometimes been emotionally conflicted, they have been deep and meaningful. I enjoy what learning about and being connected to Korea has brought me. I like wearing a *hanbok*. Still, I am not an authority on Korea. I don't speak on behalf of Koreans or as though I were Korean. Most importantly, I have tried to have the sensitivity to notice when boundaries are shifting around me.

There still are times when the boundaries of adopted adults and parents of young adopted children cross. Adoptive parents as their children's representatives in the early years can easily find themselves competing for Korean resources with adult adoptees, "wearing *hanboks*" at the right times for the younger kids in the space of the adult adoptees for whom it is the wrong time. This is what happened during the planning of the first KAAN conference. One older adult adoptee said to me, "The younger adoptees don't need to be involved. They have not suffered like we have. Their turn can come later."

Observing our community interactions, Korean American author, Helie Lee, once said to me, "Isn't Korea big enough?"

Sometimes it isn't. But, I am hopeful. As a community, adoptive parents and adoptees are growing more aware of each other's needs and boundaries. I think they can find ways to respect each other, but the understanding is something those in the adoption community have to work at.

Being Parents

One of the first things adoptive parents say to me when I suggest they participate in Friends of Korea's programs, attend a KAAN Conference, or participate in a Korean Community event is that their children are not yet "asking about Korea." They seem to feel the child will ask when he is ready, and then they will provide some information. My own experience has been that, often, young children are not able to frame the questions they have about the differences they see and sense, though the need for answers and connection is still there. There may be times when kids need a break from things Korean, but it is also likely that it may be easier for parents to minimize the issue than to confront it. Children are aware of differences. If Korea is something their parents never mention, it may be something too scary for them to mention either.

Friends of Korea has held discussion events with information about any number of things related to Korea and to adoption. At one event there was an adoptive family attending one of the meetings for the first time. The father rose and made the statement that his children were not interested in learning about their Korean heritage, but he figured they might as well come to one event and see if they liked it. He then asked about taking his kids to Korea in the future. He said he had never been to a foreign country and was concerned that Korea, "being a third world nation," might not be a safe place to visit. I was amazed. His fear of taking his kids to an event, let alone Korea, was palpable. I could not imagine his kids felt they had permission to be interested in or to like Korea. On the other hand he was there at the Friends of Korea meeting. I tried to keep judgments to the minimum and helpful comments to the maximum, in the hopes that for his kid's sake he might feel safe enough to venture out again. I believed Friends of Korea events might be helpful to his family. I know I couldn't have raised my kids alone. I needed meaningful support groups.

When my children were younger, I made the decision that they were going to have opportunities to learn about Korea. In our family, all of our children, including the one born to us, attended Korean School until they were thirteen years old. For many years, my husband and I attended as well. My sentiment was that Korea is important to everyone in this family. We are going to learn about it together. I didn't give my children a choice. This was my decision for them as their parent. My boundary was these are my children, and I am their mother; I will make decisions on their behalf. I tried to make informed judgments about my children's needs following conversations with Asian Americans, Korean Americans, and later on adult Korean-born adoptees, but they were my choices.

Adoptive parents raise their children "successfully" in a variety of different ways. Most range between the path I have taken and the fearful father I mentioned above. While we may disagree about what is the best approach, I do support the right of the parents in each family to be the parents. As long as Korea continues to engage in intercountry adoption, and agencies place Korean-born children in American homes, adoptive parents are the parents of their adopted children. They make decisions for them, right or wrong, as all parents do. In the interest of maintaining good long-term family relationships for myself, I have hoped to make more right decisions than wrong ones.

Respecting Boundaries with Adult Adoptees

In furthering my efforts to be an effective parent, I have appreciated the opportunity to consult with adult adoptees who became my friends. Only they can maturely articulate how it feels to have been adopted from another country. The "became my friends" part is important. Just as when I connected with non-adopted Asian Americans and Korean Americans, relationships with adult adoptees have worked best when they are reciprocal, meeting mutual needs. Over the years, I have not asked adoptees I casually encountered for their opinion on how to raise my children. It felt to me that to do so would be the same as when curious strangers want to have discussions about adoption in the grocery store as my children stand about like so many cabbages. There is a time and a place for such things. I have noticed some adult adoptees really enjoy serving on panels at adoption community events to field the questions of adoptive parents. Some adult adoptees want to become mentors to younger children. They are not obligated to do either of these things. It is a gift when they do them. They have the right to be just people living their lives, perhaps still discovering what their path is, not wanting to be public about private matters. I want to respect personal boundaries as well as ethnic ones. When I have been willing to respect that adoptees needs and view of the adoption experience differ from my own, there have been many chances for friendship.

Boundaries and Caucasian Siblings

In our family, as in many others, it is not the case that all of my children are adopted. Having done much to meet the needs of my two Korean-born children, I have often wondered how that focus affected my son Alexis. He doesn't talk about it much, but my Caucasian son must have had feelings under the surface. As you might note from his college essay, we gave him a family filled with difference and expected him to cope. You may also note his saying, "I adopted a little sister." Alexis' emphasis on the word "I" is something I really like. He took the process of adoption seriously. He supported the way our family was formed and coped with the challenges it brought by himself. He went to Korean school and can still ask in Korean, "Do you have a newspaper?" It is interesting what he remembers.

When he was in high school, Alexis had an English teacher who had a class project around immigration. The teacher was not neutral on the subject and was encouraging students to talk about the negative ways immigration was impacting the United States. My son, as the brother of two immigrants, was under pressure. On one level, my son wanted to ignore the situation and get a good grade. He could have done that. His connection to immigration was not visible to this teacher. On another level, he had family loyalty, and indeed his own integrity, to maintain. In the end, he took in a *Time* magazine with a cover story on the positive contributions of immigrants to give to his teacher, offering her the opportunity to explore a different perspective.

If Euro-American adoptive parents struggle to see how Korea fits into their lives and what the boundaries are, certainly those children born into the family also struggle. They are expected to value things Korean in support of the family, but certainly they can feel the strains of their own ethnic boundaries. Adopted kids had no choice in being the "different ones" in their families, but children born into adoptive families didn't have the choice about being in "different" families either. Euro-American kids with adopted siblings are in situations where they are called upon to maintain the family loyalty and to stick up for their siblings. They need support to do that.

Not only the general public, but also some Koreans and Korean Americans, focus in more quickly on adopted kids with special greetings due to their shared ethnicity. Being so visibly different, my adopted kids have always drawn more interest from strangers. I have wondered how that felt for my non-adopted son, who may have suffered because the spotlight was, and also was not, upon him.

Friends of Korea programs have always been for not only adoptive families, but for anyone wanting a Korean heritage connection. In the case of the core group of adoptive families, whole families, including the Euro-American siblings of adoptees, are welcome. We have occasionally had Korean American volunteers in our programs who have quite innocently shown more enthusiasm for being with adoptees than for being with the non-adopted siblings of adoptees. Excited to have the opportunity to connect with adoptees, Korean Americans sometimes zoom in on them. In one case two sisters, one blonde and blue-eyed, the other with brown hair and brown eyes stood waiting to meet their new Korean school teacher. The teacher went directly to the brown-eyed sister with whom she shared an ethnicity and began to stroke her hair in greeting. Her blonde sister stood next to her with an "I don't know what I am doing here" look on her face. The Korean American teacher then took the adoptee's hand and led her into the classroom, without a glance at her sister. This Caucasian sister of an adoptee, expected to maintain the family loyalty, felt quite out of place. My fear was that this Euro-American sibling might develop negative feelings about Korea, which could interfere with her understanding of and relationship with her adopted sibling. I notice when they are young, the Caucasian siblings participate as fully in Friends of Korea programs as their Korean-born siblings do. Over the years, the participation shifts. In Friends of Koreas teen programs, all the kids are Korean-born. My hope is that someday the adoption community can also find the time and space to fully address the adoption related needs of children in adoptive families who are not adopted.

Certainly Alexis is not Korean, but when Koreans and Korean Americans have acknowledged him as an important member of our family, I believe it has been helpful. I have greatly appreciated that folks like Chong Hui Ryner, Eyoungoo Park, Denise Park, Youngseo Jang, Luke Kim, and Grace Kim have shown interest in all the children who make up adoptive families, including those born into their families. Alexis, who is now married, brought his wife Elaine on a trip to Korea. He felt that because she had become a member of this family, it was important for her to know about Korea. Alexis told me he still struggles with two things. He wants to know how to view his own ethnicity positively and productively. He wants to have an acknowledgement that he is "part Korean." While he understands the boundaries of his siblings being more Korean, Korea has played a large role in his life. He wants that connection acknowledged into his adulthood.

Alexis is connected to Korea. He wears his Korea jacket in March 1988, and strolls through Myung Dong with Mark in summer 2004.

Interactions between Ethnic Koreans and Adoptive Parents

Once I was given the opportunity to write an article translated into Korean for the *Korea Times*, where I had the opportunity to share my feelings and sensitivities with Koreans and Korean Americans, in the hopes they would be less likely to step on my boundaries. I decided to focus on the words Koreans and Korean Americans use that have been hard for me to hear. I wrote the following piece:

The Words We Use

When talking to adoptive families the words Korean Americans use are very important. At one time, a reporter in Korea wrote an article in which he talked about an adoptee who was searching for her "real parents." In the same article he praised her "foster parents" for bringing her up well. He meant to be kind, yet when adoptive families associated with KAAN read this article in the *KAAN newsletter*, they sent me comments like the following one: "Regarding the reference to the article on the adoptee who was searching for her 'real parent.' If the birthmother is her real mother, what is her adoptive mother!? I am an adoptive mother and I am real, and I am not a foster parent."

Adoptive mothers consider themselves to be the real mothers of their Korean-born children. In addition to me, her American mother, my daughter also has a Korean mother. She is also her real mother. My daughter can enjoy learning about her genetic history and building a relationship with her birth family. It is not a contest between us. But, I hope Koreans are aware the nature of adoptees' relationships with their adoptive parents and with their birth parents is different. Adoptive parents did not step in when they adopted their children to take the place of birth parents. Birth parents do not step in later in the adoptee's life and take the place of the adoptive parents. The adoptee has two families, and both are real.

Adoptive parents are also not foster parents. In the U.S., foster parents are temporarily responsible for children placed in their care when the children's birth parents cannot care for them. This relationship may last a few months or years. Of course foster parents may come to feel deeply for children in their care, but they are not adoptive parents. Adoption is a permanent relationship. In our family I expect to be the grandmother to the children of all of my children, including the two who are adopted from Korea. I expect they will continue to interact with, visit, relate to, and love me, even when I am quite old. I expect to feel the same way about them. And, I expect when I die, all three of them will inherit equally from my estate. I think most Korean Americans like to reach out to adoptive families. It will go smoother if they use the words adoptive parent instead of foster parent and birth parent instead of real parent.

While I would like Koreans and Korean Americans to acknowledge the depth of my connection between my children and myself, I also accept Koreans' feelings about interethnic adoption may be different than mine. How must it feel for Koreans to see Korean children in white families? So far the Korean government has chosen to send children in need of families out for adoption in other countries, but clearly they have done so with mixed feelings. I mentioned that in 1998 President Kim Dae Jung invited adoptees on a "Feel and Touch Motherland Tour," during which he apologized to them for having sent them abroad for adoption. My strongest impression is Koreans care what has become of the 100,000 plus children who left their birth country for adoption. You can hear it expressed in the following excerpt from the videotape First Lady, Lee Hee Ho sent to us for the first KAAN conference.

"Members of KAAN and officials with the first national conference, first I congratulate you for the opening of the first national conference of KAAN, which I believe is deeply significant. I would like to be personally attending the conference and exchanging greetings with you if I could. And, I am sorry to have to join you only through this video message. In Korea, and when I visited the United States, I have often had the opportunity to meet with members of the adoptive families of Korean children. I am always moved and am grateful whenever I watch the Korean children who are growing up happily and in good health with the adoptive families.

I would like to take this opportunity to applaud and praise the Korean adoptees that have grown up into such fine young persons, brimming with courage and hope. At the same time, I am deeply grateful to the adoptive parents who have brought Korean adoptees up in a warm family atmosphere, doing their best and inspiring courage indeed. I respect you very much. Looking back, the Korean War that broke out forty-nine years ago caused tremendous pain for all Koreans. It placed huge trials, especially on the children who wandered around amid the ruins of war, having lost their parents.

At that time, the Korean people had to send the Korean children who had lost their parents overseas, and most of them were adopted in the United States. Of course, they were also sent overseas for adoption because of the customs and ways of thinking which made Koreans traditionally avoid adoption. While sending more than 140,000 children for adoption, Koreans have been feeling shame and a sense of guilt. There has also been a lot of self-reflection over the fact that we could not bring up our own children ourselves."

I have commented previously about feeling uncomfortable when Koreans thank me for adopting "their" children. I have been having second thoughts about those concerns. I am thinking Koreans and Korean Americans belong in a different category from the general public who feel I have done a "good thing" by adopting children into our families. This is because Koreans and Korean Americans are not neutral bystanders in the process. They have their own emotional needs and their own boundaries. When they say "thank you," I am pretty sure I am not hearing all of the underlying meaning. I'd like to respect the fact that as I am entitled to my feelings, Koreans are entitled to their underlying feelings which belong to them and are not mine to pick at and probe.

I have read in several articles that some Canadians feel children of African ancestry born in the United States and adopted into Canada will do better there because there is less racism in Canada. I think about how I feel when I read that. Of course I feel happy when I hear any child has a home where they are loved and are offered opportunities to grow and achieve. But, if I were to say "thank you" to Canadians, I might also be wondering if thinking "race doesn't matter" in Canada isn't a bit naïve. Because of cultural differences, this example of Canadians adopting children born in the U. S. may not exactly mirror Americans adopting Korean children. It does illustrate that when adoptions are occurring between two countries, the adoptions may be viewed differently in each of those two countries. Koreans have their own set of feelings about the children leaving their shores for adoption out of the country. Adoptees speaking from their life experience have a variety of opinions. I feel a definite boundary would be crossed if I were to speak for Koreans about whether or not children should be leaving Korea for adoption overseas. There are adopted adults who feel strongly that adoption from Korea should continue. Some of them have made it a career choice to work for adoption agencies. There are other adopted adults who feel strongly that Korean children should remain in Korea. As an adoptive parent, I can have an opinion, but from my perspective, dialogue about the future of these adoptions belongs among Koreans themselves and with the adoptees that experienced them. Ultimately, the future of Korean children is up to the Korean government to decide.

Dealing with All the Boundaries

When do Koreans, Korean Americans, adoptees or adoptive parents get to be completely comfortable about adoption? Dealing with adoption issues and the coming together from differing perspectives is about stretching and growing, not about avoiding the slightest discomfort. Sometimes I hear families with young children from Korea or families with children from China say they are not going to repeat the mistakes of the parents who raised the "first-generation" of Korean-adopted adults. Within the adoption community the "first-generation" of Korean adoptees refers to those who were placed for adoption in the United States from 1955 through 1980 (approximately). It is a good thing to learn from those who come before and make forward progress. Yet, I would say to those adoptive parents who are raising the next generation of adoptees, "You will make some of the mistakes made by the adoptive parents who came before you as well as different ones. It is in the nature of being parents."

At age eighteen, David once said in anger, "After I leave, I don't know if I will continue this relationship."

I replied, "You know you can move across the country and never speak to me again, but we will still be related. I raised you. You are my son. I am inside of you, and you are inside of me." I will always be the mother of three children. This will be true no matter the quality of the relationship. It will be true no matter who acknowledges it.

Although this was something David said in anger, and it is not his current view, I mention it because I feel it relates to those adoptees and adoptive families who have had to let go of each other, and who may yet achieve a better understanding. I know several parents of adult adoptees whose children I watched grow. A few have made the transition to adulthood seamlessly. In other families with good parents who loved their children and tried to give them connections to their heritage, the transition to adulthood has included struggle and sometimes a break in family ties. Adoptees may be angry over what they have lost. They may search for birth parents. They may return to live in Korea. They may change their names. One adoptee shared a story of estrangement from her adoptive family. Her family had difficulty in accepting her thoughts and feelings. Having strong ideas about the career she should choose and the way she ought to live her life, they had difficulty giving her the freedom to explore. She ended the relationship. A few years later, she was at a point of in her life where she was considering reaching out to her parents. It was at this time her parents contacted her and let her know they no longer considered her their daughter. If adoptees do let go of their adoptive parents, a door can be kept open, so they can come back. Relationships evolve over time. I have also known adult adoptees in their late twenties, thirties, and forties who have completed a cycle and reconnected with their adoptive families.

New parents are full of hope, but over time, being parents in any situation involves letting go of fantasies of how children should be and accepting them as they are. This is no less true with the added complexity of interethnic and intercountry adoption issues. I found that expecting to avoid the complexities adoption brought to my life was not realistic.

Expecting my children to accommodate to fit my needs puts a tremendous burden on them and on me too. In the end, my children who have become young adults will be who they are and confront what they must confront as they live their own lives. I have faith in their capabilities and dreams. I am going to continue to enjoy watching them as they claim their future.

A Euro-American on a Korean Tour at a Thai Restaurant in China

등잔 밑이 어둡다

Underneath the base of the lamp is dark.
KOREAN PROVERB

A Trip to China

In August 2002, I had an opportunity to explore my feelings about the meaning of Koreanness in my children's lives and in my own. I accompanied adoptees and adoptive families on the Friends of Korea Family Exchange Program trip to Korea. After having safely sent the participants home, I remained. I had been offered the opportunity to join a Korean tour group traveling to China. I brought into the mix all of my previous experiences as well as my life experience of being an adoptive mother of Korean-born children. I was the only Caucasian on a tour for Koreans.

The tour, organized by a Korean travel agency, catered to the needs of Koreans interested in visiting Beijing, which is a one-and-a-half-hour plane ride from Seoul. Similar to tours organized by American travel agencies for Americans to visit other countries, this tour was designed to keep the particular needs of the Korean clientele in mind, promising such things as at least one Korean meal each day and a Korean-speaking tour guide.

I was not fluent in Korean, but with some rudimentary knowledge of Korean language and culture, I was sure I could get by. As the tour progressed I did find that, along with Chinese, most of the sites had signs in English, which were helpful when I had trouble following the guide's Korean explanation. The trip was a wonderful chance to broaden my perspective.

Korean Chinese—What Makes Someone Korean?

I hoped the trip would afford me the opportunity to get to know "different kinds" of Koreans better and build more of an understanding of how Koreans view the world. Having joined a Korean tour group, I saw China from a Korean perspective. In doing so, I learned very little about China. Instead I learned about the perspective of Korean tourists in China. I felt this was important because adoptees sometimes express a sense of not being "real" Koreans. What makes someone "authentic"? Are Koreans living in China "real" Koreans? What about Koreans living in Russia? What is the essence of Koreanness that makes someone "real"? By looking at all the sorts of ways one can be Korean, I thought that maybe I would better understand by contrast which are the Korean elements in adoptees, and even within the other non-Korean members of my own family.

Whatever country adoptees come from, their search for the essence of identity occurs in a similar manner. A child adopted from South America is Hispanic, but as Jean Nelson explains in her book, *Butterflies in the Wind*, they come from particular countries in Latin America. All Hispanics are not the same. Adoptees from Latin America sort out the essence of who they are by bouncing against the differences between other Latin American countries and their own particular Latin American country of origin. How are adoptees who came to the United States from Taiwan different than those who came from the mainland of China? How are they different from Chinese Americans? Exploring those differences will help adoptees from China find a better sense of who they are. David wants to visit Japan. Though people from Japan look like him, how are they different from Koreans? What is the commonality of being Asian?

I pondered what conflicting loyalties ethnic Koreans living in China experience. Did they consider themselves Koreans or Chinese or Korean Chinese? Our Korean tour guide was a third-generation ethnic Korean living in China. I find it hard to imagine many Korean Americans, fluent in Korean, whose grandparents immigrated to the United States from Korea. On our trip we met many fully bilingual Korean Chinese who were third-generation. How could this be possible? What caused them to be separate enough in Chinese society to keep their Korean heritage so much intact? Was this a good thing or a bad thing? Did that feeling vary depending upon the circumstances? Our guide did tell us he was a member of the Communist Party. He spent much of his time chatting in Chinese with the bus driver who didn't speak Korean.

Because our tour was designed to cater to Koreans, and translation from Chinese to Korean was necessary, we met a lot of people who were Korean Chinese. I was told ninety percent of those visiting China are Korean. When not rolling along the streets competing with bicycles, their tour busses filled huge parking lots. Because Koreans are important to China's emerging economy, Korean Chinese are important. We met them in Korean restaurants, herbal medicine stores, a pearl factory, and anywhere a Korean tourist might visit, where a Korean Chinese liaison with knowledge of both languages and cultures would come in handy.

The Korean Chinese were different from the Chinese we met. Perhaps out of some sense of bonding with the Koreans on our tour, they acted more familiarly in sharing knowledge of Korea. Yet, they were different than the Koreans I was with. Our Korean guide had never visited Korea. What he knew of Korea came from what he had heard from others who shared his ethnicity. He maintained a bit of aloofness from the group. At one point we offered him a popsicle, which he declined. This might have been for any number of reasons. I thought the primary reason might be that he wanted to maintain his position as tour guide, being careful not to favor any of the group members over other group members. Maybe he didn't like popsicles. Some Koreans on our tour didn't see it that way. They offered another explanation. They said, "He is too proud as a Chinese to take things from us." Our guide had a different connection to Korea than the travelers I was with. While our guide was ethnically Korean, the Koreans in our group saw him as Chinese. Though he was third-generation living among them, it was clear the Chinese saw our tour guide as Korean. For Korean Chinese their ethnicity and cultural history mattered. To what degree it mattered, and in what ways, only they could say. But there was no doubt it mattered.

As I think of Korean Chinese, Korean Americans, and of Korean American adoptees, I am struck by the fact that their Koreanness never ceases to be a part of who they are. Yet, "being Korean" means different things in different sets of people. Korean ethnicity matters sometimes because of expectations from the outside of a person and, sometimes, because of expectations from within. There has been a flood of Korean emigrants, going to countries all over the globe, who are in some ways defined by the life-altering fact of having left Korea. I feel connected to them. As their lives have intertwined with mine, they have changed who I am. Especially the lives of two Korean adoptees, who happen to be my son and daughter, have changed who I am. Yet the experiences of Korean emigrants are different from each other in as many ways as they are different from my experience. They don't walk in each other's shoes either. Despite that, they are all in some sense Korean.

Are You a Member of This Group?

It is somewhat unusual for a Euro-American to join a group of Koreans traveling to China. I wondered about how accepted I would be as a member of the group. Acceptance as a member of the group seemed to have two components: one acceptance by the group itself, two acceptance of group membership from those outside the group. I needed to achieve both of these components to feel a full-fledged part of the group.

Membership within the group, as seen by the group, was not immediate. There were some stares at first, but these were overcome I think because I joined the group with a Korean American friend. The fact that someone Korean considered me a friend put me in a different category almost immediately. There was a second factor that was helpful as well. I do have some limited knowledge of language and culture, which led me to act in ways that allowed others in the group to feel comfortable. I was willing to engage in all the group activities: eat Korean food, interact in Korean the best I could, and get to know the members of the group as individuals. I noticed some Koreans who did not have entirely positive perceptions of Americans were still able to accept me. One man had stories to share about his trip to the United States. He talked about keeping his hand in his pocket at all times, so he wouldn't be robbed. He then said that had been a bad idea because that showed the pickpockets exactly where he was carrying his money. The more he talked, the more it seemed as if he had been robbed in America. But, when I asked, he told me he hadn't been robbed. No one he knew had been robbed. He hadn't witnessed any robberies. He seemed full of stereotypes about America and seemed to expect an experience that matched his preconceptions. Yet, he seemed to like me. As far as Americans go, I believe he thought I was one of the "good ones."

I felt my experience of being accepted within this Korean group might reflect those experiences of my Korean-born children's acceptance by some of their fellow Americans. I have heard my son's stories about peers and teachers who, while they accepted him, felt quite free to share stereotypical perceptions of Asians with him. Perhaps they are praising him for not being one of "those" Asians. I had some sense of how this must feel to him, since I wanted to convey to those I was with that America was not a violent lawless place. My children, it seems, have become able to sort out those people that share stereotypical perceptions with malice and those who do so in ignorance. I found myself doing the same thing in sorting out stereotypical perceptions about Americans within my tour group.

The second challenge to my membership in the group came from outside the group. Sometimes I was challenged when entering palaces or other points of interest. The tour guide would go ahead and pay for all of us. As we entered, the Chinese ticket takers would count us off. When it was my turn, an arm would extend barring my way as their eyes rolled toward the tour guide, who would then confirm my membership in this Korean group.

I took it in stride, not letting it ruin my day, and savoring the feeling of it. I thought it was the closest I would come to standing in the shoes of my Korean-born children whose membership in our family is sometimes challenged. Yet it was mildly annoying, because no matter how many times it happened, I would forget to expect it. It came as an interruption in the smooth flow of my tourist experience. I had been accepted within the group as a member of the group by the group. Though the group was protective of me, we all knew that I was unusual. I was enjoying being a part of the group sightseeing together, when the abruptness of this challenge to my group membership would occur. It was jarring, not quite letting me be free to just enjoy the trip.

Clearly, I couldn't hide from the fact the skin I was in mattered. My membership within the group, as assessed by those outside it, was never a given. I didn't look like I belonged, and people are often not sure what to do with the unusual. People would question me, needing me to help them make sense of and explain this discrepancy in their world. At home when in a store or other public place with my Korean-born adopted kids, we get asked if my child is an exchange student. It has the same caught up short feeling as what I experienced in China when my membership in the group was challenged.

There are some major divergences, though, between the short trip I took to China and my children's lifelong journey. The distinction is that I personally chose to be the "different one" in a Korean group. It was for a period of three days total. When I was challenged, it was not my membership in

Chris in China.

my own family that was being challenged. I was an adult and not a child having this experience. I have a personality that is fairly outgoing, causing me to relish culturally challenging exposure. I don't particularly mind being noticed. My children did not choose to be adopted. The duration of their experience is lifelong. It is their membership in their own family that is being challenged. Neither of the children we adopted enjoys being "onstage."

For these reasons my adventure in China is distinctly different than my children's everyday lives. This difference contributes to the variation in my perspective from that of my children. I didn't write this book to tell my children's stories; it is their right to speak with their own voice. Their memories and perceptions sometimes parallel mine, but they also diverge from mine. The only story each of us can ever fully tell is our own.

Famous Chinese Medical Clinic—Americans Are Trouble Makers.

I was excited to visit China. I was focused on the size and scale of the Great Wall and the Forbidden City, which made the grandeur of ancient China evident, especially against the sharp contrast of the poverty of the current inhabitants. So many beggars and vendors greeted our bus at every stop. They were willing to accept any currency. American dollars, Korean Won, and Chinese Yuan could all be used in bargaining. Despite scenes of poverty, it was clear China is working to reclaim her former grandeur. If there is a tall building, it is a modern, comfortable hotel. The airport gleams. The highways are being reconstructed right under the wheels of the endless busses.

Because of the group I was with, I was also focused on the Korean tourist experience. Tourism seems to be one of China's roads to the future. The Chinese government is making the most of it. In addition to the obvious tourist destinations, at least for Korean tourists, there are some "required stops" to encourage the spending of money in China. We went to a jade factory, a tea shop, a pearl factory, an herbal medicine shop and more, all specifically tailored to Korean tourists. We ate at government restaurants with shopping opportunities included. From my perspective the most puzzling "required stop" we visited was the Famous Chinese Medical Clinic. At this stop, which we were told was world renowned, we could see pictures of all sorts of famous folks who had been treated there. We were taken to a fairly small room for our group of twenty and told that the famous doctors would consult with each member of our group. The doctors would offer suggestions for relief of any ailments from which we might be suffering. While we were waiting, we were offered back massages for two dollars each.

Because I was an American, I was interpreting this experience in an American way. In my mind, it was hard to imagine tour groups coming into the United States and rolling up to Johns Hopkins, for example, to be seen for a consultation with famous doctors for free. I felt embarrassed for China that this was something the government would consider "showing off." There was more going on here, though. This was not a site necessarily for U.S. visitors to China. It was a site for Korean visitors to China. My impulse was to be polite.

While I couldn't step out of the skin I was in, I wasn't here only as an American. I was here as part of this Korean tour group. As I had been accepted by the group, I also took on the group's feelings as one of its members. Everyone in our Korean tour had heard about and was anticipating this stop. As their comments about it were translated to me, it was clear they were expecting a negative experience. They were feeling coerced into this experience. So, it was there the rowdy American nature of me and my Korean American friend, with whom I had joined the group, asserted itself. Picking up on the group's mood, the situation became ludicrous to me and to my Korean American friend, who began to rub the shoulders and beat on the back of the person in front. We were avoiding the two-dollar charge by doing the massages ourselves. Soon we were all doing it in a line, until we turned and did it to the person behind us, so that the people on both ends got a turn. The cross-cultural nature of the experience was interesting to me. We were doing Korean massage, but the independent nature of us two Americans was certainly infecting the group members, causing them to act out their feelings in a more direct manner. Maybe you could say we were doing Korean massage in American style. The Koreans I was with were affecting my American behavior and feelings. My Korean American friend and I were affecting the way those feelings were expressed.

When you join a group, you bring something of your cultural background and life experience to the group, affecting the nature of the group dynamic. The staff of the Famous Chinese Medical Clinic did not finish our free consultations before throwing us out, without showing us the medicine we could purchase to cure what ailed us. Though my original intent was to be polite, my cultural background had come out. We are who we are. I did have a thought of Korean adoptees returning to their motherland, bringing their Americanness with them. When our children visit Korea, they do so as who they have become. That may include some American assertiveness and rebelliousness. It is also true my children brought Koreanness to our family. They have changed who I am. Had I been the parent of a child adopted from China, my impulse to be polite might have been uppermost. Because of my children, my loyalty tended to be more toward the feelings of the Koreans I was with.

Bonding with Other Caucasians—The American Baseball Group

Although I was captivated by my visit to China and was very comfortable with my new Korean friends, I did find myself longing to see other Caucasians. I did not see many Americans, and on those few occasions when I did see other Caucasians at tourist sites, they were as likely to be speaking Spanish, Russian, French, or German as they were to be speaking English. The question that puzzled me was what kind of experience did Euro-Americans, who visited China as a group, have? Did they have a set of restaurants, and sites, such as the Famous Chinese Medical Clinic, especially for them as the Koreans did, but from a perspective that the Chinese felt would interest Americans? Did the Chinese have a different set of tour destinations for the Spanish or the Russians? Other than groups for Americans adopting Chinese children, there didn't seem to be groups for Americans and Europeans, as most often the Caucasians I did see were on their own. One couple from England told me that it had been really quite difficult to make their way around and find what they wanted to see. Apparently, Europeans and Americans do not come to visit China in as great a number as the Koreans do. At that point I was quite happy I had my Korean group to relate to. Then one morning we ran into the American baseball group. This group had come to Seoul, Korea, to play baseball with Korean teams. They were making a side trip to China. My interest in them was not only to learn what sort of experience they were having, but also in having the chance to share with someone who had a background similar to mine. There was some comfort in learning that the woman I talked to was from Walnut Grove, California, and she knew where my home, El Dorado Hills, California, was.

Once my Korean-born son was pondering what sort of girl he might be likely to choose if he were to marry. He was frustrated because some Koreans he knew did not seem to find him Korean enough. Despite that, he told me if he ever got married, that he was going to marry someone Asian. He asked me if I thought it was racist that he didn't want to consider marrying someone Caucasian. I told him it probably depended on his reason.

He said, "It's comfort level, Mom."

When I had this need to connect with other Caucasians in China, I thought I had a glimpse of what he meant. He wanted to be with others who looked like him.

Euro-American on a Korean Tour at a Thai Restaurant in China

During our trip to China I found a metaphor for my life experience as the adoptive parent of Korean American kids. We had been promised on our tour one Korean meal a day. From my perspective as an American, we *only* had Korean food in China. On the one hand I didn't mind, because I like Korean food and had been eating it for two weeks prior in Korea. On the other hand I did mind, because I really had wanted to experience authentic Chinese food in China. What was very interesting was the other members of my Korean group were sure they were having Chinese food.

I was not able to unravel the difference in our perspectives until we went to a Thai restaurant in China. When they brought out food, virtually indistinguishable from what we had been eating at every other meal, I confronted my Korean American friend, who assured me we were indeed having Thai food. I looked at my friend and pointed out the *kimchi*. Then it hit me. Though I knew I was having a different experience than the Koreans I was with, I was, without meaning to, expecting our experience to be the same. Suddenly I had this discrepancy to resolve. The Koreans I was with all thought they were eating Thai food. Since I was the only one who was seeing it differently, was I wrong? Or could we all be right? Were we seeing the world differently because of who we were?

Traditional Korean lamp drawn by Eyoungsoo Park.

I remembered the Korean proverb: "Underneath the base of the lamp is dark."

Long ago in Korea, Korean lamps hung with light pouring out above and around them. There was no light under the base of the lamp, which was solid. The proverb's meaning is that we often can't see what is right in front of us. The Thai food I ate and loved in California was likely not Thai food either. What we had been eating in China was Chinese food and Thai food cooked for Korean taste buds. The subtlety was lost on me. It all tasted Korean. I realized what I ate in California was Chinese and Thai foods cooked for American taste buds. Since I have never eaten Thai food with Thai friends in Thailand, nor Chinese food in China with Chinese folks, perhaps I have never really eaten either of them.

What gave me some comfort was that I didn't think anyone in our Korean group had ever really had Thai food or Chinese food either. I was having the experience of a Euro-American on a Korean tour at a Thai Restaurant in China. This was very uniquely the only experience that I could have. I realized had my children been with me, they, as Korean American adoptees, would have been having an experience all their own, which would certainly be different than mine. It would have been the only experience they could have from the shoes in which they stood, the experience inherent from their life situation. My children neither stand in my shoes nor look out through my eyes.

Koreans in China

When I showed the first draft of this book to my Korean American friend, I had written as follows:

Despite my trying to see the world through their eyes, the Koreans I was with were having their own unique experience in China that I could barely touch. Recently Korea had hosted the world soccer matches. It had been a national frenzy in which the Korean team had performed well, and Korea itself had shone as a progressive country hosting the world. You would be hard-pressed to find a Korean who did not own a red shirt, the color of the Korean soccer team, with the words "Be the Reds" on it in English.

As our tour rolled through China, I looked at the scores of other Korean tours also visiting. There were Korean school groups, Korean community groups, Korean Cub Scouts, and groups such as ours with folks of all ages in them. Whole groups of Korean kids went by in their red soccer shirts. As we floated through a scenic gorge formed by a dam, boatloads of Korean tourists passed us on their way back upstream. We all smiled and waved at each other. Then the boat of Korean kids let out the soccer cheer, "Dae Han Min Kuk!" (Korea). The Koreans seemed to be taking over China in their red shirts.

I wondered if their cheer wasn't a bit inappropriate, as this was China and not Korea. Koreans seemed to feel powerful in China, which has for centuries been dominant like big brother to Korea. We had a foot massage one evening after dinner. It was a group activity and the Koreans seemed to feel something in the fact the Chinese would even rub their feet."

"There are problems with your description," My Korean American friend said. "You don't have the full impact of it."

"How is that?" I asked.

"The national frenzy was not because Korea performed well in a soccer match. They did well enough, but whether they won or lost is not the point."

"Tell me what you see," I said.

After listening I began writing again, hoping this time that I could climb out of my well far enough to give a better description. In the 2002 World Cup Soccer matches, Korea hosted the world. They were not a "progressive" country. They were not still a "developing" country. Korea had made it to the top. It is like New York being the host of the United Nations. Korea was at the top, hosting the world. We were in a beautiful gorge in China. As we walked up to it, Chinese beggars pushed at us with their hands out. Others with something to sell came forward with crude little carvings and home made items. Mighty China was like this! Koreans had pocketfuls of money. They were on top of the world! Koreans come from a country that was once destroyed and dominated, but they have risen, not just to being okay, but to being on the top of the world.

Have I succeeded in describing it yet? Perhaps not, because, not being Korean, it is hard to do the scene justice. I realize I don't have the background to understand the depth of relationship being expressed in these tours or the feelings of either the Koreans or the Chinese. I let myself be content knowing I had been privileged to have been accepted by my Korean tour group so that they would share their viewpoint with me.

Whether it is Korean adoptees in the United Stated, Koreans in China, or a Euro-American on a Korean tour in China, each of us has a unique cultural and ethnic history that affects our feelings and actions. When you bring individual personality, distinctive experience, and life roles, such as being an adoptive parent, into the mix, each individual can only truly understand his own experience. My trip to China was a chance to explore differences in worldview and perceptions and to realize both intellectually and viscerally that the skin I am in, my ethnic and cultural history, matter.

Experience, Processing, and Memory

As I wrote this book, sharing my experience as an adoptive parent I shared what I wrote with my now-adult adoptee children. I told my story and not theirs, but because certain events I related included all of us, I wanted them to be comfortable with what I had shared. I expected that because of our different perspectives we would have experienced events differently. I was stunned to find out some of our fundamental memories and certainly our processing of events differed as well.

Diana doesn't remember there was a time she wrote Diana Eun Jung Lee Winston on all of her fourth grade papers. She doesn't remember several essays she wrote with phrases such as, "I don't know where I was born, so I am going to say I was raised by wolves."

"I want you to show me that in my own handwriting," she said.

Since I had saved those papers, I could do that. She doesn't remember her dream or the Kim left off her birthday cake that my husband and I remember. How could she? She was asleep while dreaming, and we fixed the cake before she saw it. These events are from my perspective. She does remember there was a time she really wanted to find her birthmother and was experiencing emotional turmoil, but the events that highlight that for her are different than the ones that convinced me of her need. I have included my memories of these incidents because they were my motivations for the actions I took, my window on what seemed to be happening inside her head.

In a talk with David, I asked him if he remembered the one time he had attended culture camp. He said he did.

I asked him, "Tell me what you remember."

"It was fun," he said.

"It was fun?" I repeated.

"Yeah, I went with Kendall, right? And I made friends with other kids."

I was floored. My recollection was David had not had fun at culture camp. In fact, he had wanted to go home badly enough that we'd had discussions about it with the camp's director. Whose memory is accurate? Perhaps they both are.

Not only can we not stand in someone else's shoes, we also do not stand in the same shoes ourselves throughout our lives. The ones I wore in earlier years are too tight. I have grown and processed my own memories. Memory is based not only on what we felt or thought important at the time, but what we think or feel is important now, on how we process our experiences. I think about the stories my own mother has about events that concern both her and me, how I would perhaps tell them a little differently than she does. Of course she has her own perspective coming from her experience.

What may be more interesting within a family and within the adoption community itself is not which memory is correct, nor whose feelings are more valid, but that sharing occurs in a way that strengthens relationships. When I open my ears and listen without judging, at least I can get a flavor of other's experiences. In comparing what I remember with what my children remember, I don't need to be shocked that our memories and feelings are sometimes different. We are different people. The differences in experience and memory are less important than the understanding we gain from exploring those differences in experience with each other. My experience, memory, and processing are not more valid than that of my children. If my children decide to write their stories they are likely to differ from mine. That is their truth and their right.

Afterthoughts

산 너머 산이다

After climbing one mountain, another one will be before you.
KOREAN PROVERB

Being a Mom Is Great

Being a mother to my children has not been boring. So many unexpected things have happened to me in my life so far. While I am only midway through it, I feel the fullness of it already and count myself lucky that I cannot imagine a more consequential existence. What a wonderful thing to be a mother to my children. I remember being handed Alexis in the hospital the day he was born. As his eyes searched mine, I realized whatever else happened in my life, this was magical. That bright light in his eyes is still there. I don't regret having him young. I remember looking at him through the window in the hospital nursery. We got the cutest one. For the first nine years of his life he was my only child. I was afraid the bonds would be too tight for both of us without siblings. I am glad he has both a brother and a sister.

Were we to stand back in the same shoes we wore in 1988 and could walk again through the doors of the Children's Home Society of California to receive in great excitement the picture of an adorable baby girl from Korea, would we make the same decision to adopt her? You bet. Who could imagine life without Diana in it? I don't remember the other babies in the orphanage that day we met her. We got the cutest one.

What about the five-year-old we met in Korea in December 1989, the little boy who wouldn't bow to us, and who tugged at my hand and at my heart? The other children in the orphanage the day we met him are background. There is no one like David. We got the cutest one. Whether my children came to me by birth or by adoption, being their mom is great.

Transition to Adulthood

For about a month after Alexis went away to college, I found I could not walk past his room without feeling like I had been kicked in the stomach. I appeared to be bleeding internally, much worse than when I had left him alone on his first day in kindergarten. I was really surprised at feeling so bruised, battered, and emotionally exhausted, because Alexis was ready to be on his own, and I knew it. In many ways, as is typical with mothers and their high school seniors, we had been chaffing from rubbing against each other, struggling for some time with the control issues that come before independence. I was ready for him to be on his own as well. So I was utterly surprised to be feeling so wrung out. In a phone call with my own mother, I shared how I was feeling.

"One of the worst days in my life was when I left you at the University of Texas," she said.

"Really? It was one of the best days in my life," I replied.

Ah perspective.

David is in his last semester of community college before he transfers to his four-year university. Having always played the piano by ear, David often fills our house with music, accompanying his mood. When he leaves, I am going to miss knowing how he feels. Luckily for me, Diana will be with us a bit longer, easing my letting go process. Yet, despite the feel of it for me, as I embrace my life, I want my children to embrace theirs. When I see them struggle to do that, seeming to be stuck, I worry. This may mean it is a good thing I don't know how they are feeling all the time. I wanted to live my life in a way I wouldn't regret, and so far I have. I don't regret my life, not because it has been easy, but because many times it hasn't been. I don't regret because mostly I have been able to find the resources to meet my children's needs. I don't regret it because I am living it, owning it, finding sparkle from the depth of experience I enjoy and from relationships. I want no less for my children, but such a life is not mine to give them. The life I think best for them may not be the life they want.

Conclusions

Diana tells me she is not planning on marrying or becoming a mother, but if she changes her mind, if she ever becomes a mother, she is thinking of adopting an Irish girl.

"Or maybe I will marry an Irish man and give birth to an Irish girl," she says, seemingly playing with her identity.

"What about a Korean girl?" I ask her.

"Naw, we have enough of those," she says.

She says it lightly, and I try to take it at face value, without my mind racing off into deeper analysis, remembering an adult adoptee friend who once said to me, "Adoptive parents have no sense of humor."

Adoptive parents can go crazy trying to do everything right, a course that can result in doing many things wrong. Perhaps this is true of parents generally, because it is also true when I think of Alexis. The bind adoptive parents are in is that they can also be wrong by not listening carefully enough. The free association from Diana's comments continues to take me in all directions. Koreans don't adopt Irish girls. I am reminded of a book I read called *The Great Arizona Orphan Abduction* by Linda Gordon. She describes an incident in 1904 when New York nuns brought forty Irish orphans to Arizona to be placed with Catholic families for adoption. The Catholic families happened to be Mexican. To the few white families in the area, this was unthinkable. They staged a "rescue" that was a kidnapping, and they got away with it, adopting the orphans themselves. Why is it acceptable for those of European ancestry to adopt children of color and not acceptable for people of color to adopt children of European ancestry? The fact adoptions continue to flow only in one direction is an issue we have to think about. I can't say "race doesn't matter" until the day when it is just as likely that people of color adopt children of European ancestry as the other way around. My advice to anyone considering an intercountry adoption, "Don't enter into an intercountry adoption if you are not emotionally ready to confront the concept of race and be rocked to your core."

There are challenges within the Korean American Community again in Sacramento. It appears that the new principal at the Korean School of Sacramento has tried to hire away Friends of Korea's dance teacher. In my frustration, I forget my own advice about over-generalizing. I forget I may not know all the details. I talk with one Korean American friend.

"I hate Koreans!" I tell her. Instantly I regret saying it.

"You can't say that," comes the reply.

"Well you don't like them either," I answer sheepishly.

She laughs.

But, because she is Korean she can say it, and because I am not Korean I can't. I tell her this seems unfair. She cannot disconnect from Koreans because she is Korean. I can't disconnect either, because my children are Korean, and I love them. She comes back at me with that.

"Your kids are Korean and you love them," she says.

"You are Korean, and I love you too," I say.

"Poor Chris," she says, "I think you need a hug. Can we have dinner next week?"

There is so much emotion. Once on a plane coming back from Korea, a Korean American friend was on one side of me and David was on the other.

My friend was annoyed at so many changes in Korea he wasn't sure he liked. He pointed at a young Korean guy with bleached blonde hair. "He has no pride in who he is," he said. "I hate what Korea has become."

Meanwhile David was telling me, "They have the coolest stuff in Korea. They have the best electronic games in the world. I love Korea."

I spoke to both of them. "The guy on one side of me is telling me he hates Korea. The guy on the other side of me is telling me he loves Korea. What is the white woman in the middle supposed to do?"

My Korean American friend said, "Listen, we are both telling you the same thing."

"That you will miss Korea?" I ask.

"Right."

My kids have had meaningful connections with Korean Americans. Young Seo Jang, Diana and Denise Park connect at the 2005 KAAN Conference. Grace Kim listens to a younger Diana play the piano at our house.

I miss Korea too. Maybe loving and hating is the same thing. I can never disconnect, and don't want to disconnect, from Koreans or Korean Americans. The day I adopted Diana, Korea entered my heart and soul and has grown there ever since. My friendships are real and deep enough that I can have such conversations. It has been important. My advice would be, "Don't enter into an intercountry adoption if you are not emotionally ready to make real and lasting friendships with others of your children's ethnicity."

Diana is reading this and shaking her head.

"I will be glad when you finish that book, and it is safe to talk around you again," she says.

"Is it okay to use your comments?" I ask.

"I will let you know if it is off the record," she replies.

We haven't arrived at an endpoint. Right now Alexis is sorting out if the job he got after graduation is really the job he wants. Diana is trying to figure out if she really wants to major in culinary arts when the teacher she got for "knife skills" is old with a hearing aide and yellow teeth. So far it is only lectures and cancelled classes, and she is missing the "Benihana-type chef" deboning a chicken in under a minute that she had been envisioning. As I begin to counsel David on all the steps he should be taking to decide on the right university to transfer to, he becomes irritable.

"Mom, don't worry about me." he says.

Oh, David, that is like asking the sun not to shine not to worry about all three of you. I resolve not to let it show so much.

We are in a good place right now. We have been many places before, and we may not stay here. That I know. But, I can enjoy it for the moment. My kids have their whole lives to process their memories and experiences. That processing will not be stagnant. It will be their own and not mine. Being adopted from Korea is not a one-time event, but is a part of who they